Acknowledgements

First of all, I want to thank all of the Scrum teams I've worked with in my consulting practice and, most recently, ChannelAdvisor—particularly the Product Owners. I've learned so many wonderful things about agility and how teams adapt to their contexts. It's also been incredibly enjoyable to be welcomed into these teams and be part of the energy that encompasses agile methods adoption. I'm extremely blessed to be part of each and every instance.

Secondly, I need to thank Henrik Kniberg. His _Scrum and XP from the Trenches_ book has been a true inspiration for this one. I remember when Henrik first _threw_ his book out on various discussion groups and made it freely available. I immediately downloaded a copy and it became a favorite agile reference of mine both personally and for recommending to my clients.

I found it highly practical and chock full of real-world advice—something that is often missing in many of the agile references and the community at-large. If I can provide even a small part of the value that Henrik achieved in his guide, I will be more than pleased with my efforts in giving something back to the agile community.

I also want to thank my early reviewers. To be honest with you, I'm quite nervous about releasing this into the broad agile community. I needed to get some early feedback to gain confidence. These early reviewers were gracious enough to provide time and feedback and I'm extremely grateful for every bit of it.

So a heartfelt thank you to – Carlos Alvarez, John Baker, **Tony Brill, **Shaun Bradshaw, **Michael Faisst, **Mike Hall, Margaret Menzies, **Rich Mironov, Roman Pichler and Bas Vodde;   ** - contributed 'stories' to the text, so an extra *thank you* to them.

Most importantly, I want to thank my family for putting up with yet another, albeit shorter, book project. Bug—as always, all my love and you're simply the best! To Da Boys, and Da Kids all my love too…

Contents

Chapter 1
Introduction

There are many Scrum Product Owners and/or Agile Customers who feel their job solely revolves around creating a Product Backlog or list of prioritized features for their product development efforts. While all of the agile methodologies are essentially driven by such a list, there is an incredible amount of nuance and breadth beyond this to getting the role 'right'.

I've spent the past few years working with many companies, coaching their agile teams towards more effective product development, and quite often they had adopted this attitude. Sure, the Product Owners engaged with their teams, but it wasn't always heartfelt or fully focused. Some of their common behaviors surrounded:

- Providing not much more than a high level, ordered Backlog and limited availability to the team for questions or clarification.
- User Stories were developed, but were inconsistent and refined too late—often in Sprint Planning.
- Intermittent development of Sprint Goals and rarely were they truly unique or compelling.
- Backlog grooming (maintenance) was inconsistently practiced, if practiced at all.
- The Backlogs themselves were inconsistent across teams—making organizational strategic planning and overall progress measurement quite difficult.
- Forward-looking release planning was nearly avoided—preferring *Sprint-at-a-Time* thinking.
- Little time was spent 'connecting' external stakeholders to the performance, efforts, and dynamics of their teams.

It wasn't all their faults either. They were often Product Managers within the organization who had numerous tasks that fell outside of their Scrum team responsibilities. They seemed to be conflicted with their time, focus and motivation.

As we executed Scrum across many teams and organizations, I noticed emergent patterns. Some of the teams seemed to struggle all of the time, barely completing their sprints, and often missing their overall Sprint Goals. Mark my words carefully—they failed! Geez…that's not supposed to happen within agile teams!

Conversely, some teams performed much better than others and consistently over-delivered on their promises. They often created functionality that was simple and struck to the heart of their customers' needs. Their code was straightforward and of high quality and seemed to have very few bugs. I'd even say a few of these teams ventured into the hyper-productive arena that Jeff Sutherland and others so often *illustrate* [1] as the agile *nirvana state*.

Upon closer observation a set of patterns, approaches, and techniques emerged that I believe represent the approaches, behaviors and attitudes of Great Product Owners. It is these observations that I want to share with you in this book. Clearly, not all of them will apply to you in your contexts. However, it is my hope that they will encourage you to try new approaches and/or find a renewed determination and focus in your role as a Product Manager & Owner.

The Books' Context

The title of the book emphasizes a focus of "From the Inside Out". What do I mean by that? I mean that nearly every conversation within centers on your interactions with your Agile/Scrum team first. I'm certainly not downplaying the importance of being customer or externally facing as a Product Owner. In fact, that _is_ your "Prime Directive". However, I've seen so many Agile Product Owners that that's all they do.

---

[1] Sutherland has spoken and written at length about his experiences while at PatientKeeper. He alludes to his team's achieving 200-300% performance improvements over their Waterfall counterparts.

They collaborate with customers and stakeholders; they're on the road three weeks out of four, and then, they're doing product demos the remainder of the time. All along, their teams are drowning without them! While I honor how difficult this role is, I want to emphasize the characteristics of a Great Product Owner as they engage their teams "in the moment" of Sprinting. That before you look externally, you've established a partnership with your team and are spending sufficient time with them; or at the very least, are providing the Backlog, goals, and feedback they need.

I'm also assuming that you have some basic knowledge and experience in Scrum. That you've operated as, or worked closely with, a Product Owner in creating a Product Backlog or two and seen it's execution through a Scrum team. That you've seen much of the potential within Scrum teams and see them as a means towards creating great products by collaboration and a focus on quality execution.

I'm also making the assumption, and a very generous one, that you've already defined your business and marketing goals for your Scrum project(s) so, all of that up-front work has been completed. From a marketing perspective, here are some of the things that would/should have already occurred, particularly if you're focused on _product_ development efforts—

- Defined the target market
- Identify intended customer(s) and sales channel(s)
- Clearly articulate the top few benefits
- Establish a simple version of a pricing/revenue model

This is sort of the minimal set of marketing tasks that need to be completed before tasking a Scrum team with product development work. I'm assuming that someone in the organization, perhaps the Product Manager or Product Owner, has established a sound business foundation for beginning your project.

Beyond product development, you may be working as part of an internal development function within an IT organization. While much of your focus is the same as the product focused team, you often have a somewhat captured market and revenue stream from your internal customers.

In both these cases, a *Project Charter* [2] is often established before beginning any effort. The charter often contains elements of:

- Business case and payback estimates
- Initial budget estimates
- Mission and vision; the motivation of the endeavor
- High level requirements (functional, non-functional)
- Views to constraints (schedule, cost, scope)
- Quality targets
- Architectural, design, system performance goals
- Team staffing, space and tool allocation
- Risks and contingencies

The charter establishes the baseline for the project from a working assumptions perspective. If you haven't established a formal charter, I hope you've at least considered or explored many of the above areas informally.

From the Inside Out

Again, with my "in the moment" perspective, we're not going to spend much time discussing project preparatory activity. Instead, my assumption is that you have a well understood and characterized project that has just begun implementation to leverage Scrum and Agile dynamics. So, you're essentially *diving in*.

Diving in with your initial focus being—the team. Looking to see how your role merges with theirs. Learning how to feed their Backlog and provide high quality customer feedback. Discovering their delivery capabilities and effectively managing stakeholder expectations. Providing a compelling vision for what your customers need and why they need to build it the way they are. Sharing challenges in such a way that it motivates the team with enthusiasm and energy.

Yes, you need to be customer facing and yes, you need to intimately understand their needs. But, in order to deliver towards those needs, your team is your first priority. Only they can help you deliver great products— from the inside out.

---

[2] Appendix B provides a concise overview of a 'typical' Chartering process and activity

Recommended Reading Flow

I recommend first reading the Introduction, Chapter 2, and 3 to understand the basic focus and flow for the book.

The flow of the book targets the Scrum life-cycle—moving from Backlog preparation through to end of Sprint Retrospectives. I will also touch on some leadership and scaling challenges in the later chapters. Most of the remaining chapters can stand-alone; you should be able to pick and choose what might be useful to you.

My Personal Context

It's important for me to clarify my own context in all of this. Mostly, my role has been as a Scrum Master, team member, and Agile Coach across many teams in a wide variety of organizations. I've never operated solely as a Product Owner, but certainly have assisted and partnered in the role. So, primarily, my _lens_ is that of a coach who is guiding their Scrum teams.

I'm also a certified Scrum Master Practicing (CSP) and a certified Product Owner (CSPO). I've seen and directly experienced the HUGE difference that a Product Owner who gets it 'right' vs. one that gets it 'wrong' can make. It's those observations that are driving the creation of this book in that I want to increase the 'right' side of the equation.

Most of my team experiences have been between medium sized agile instances of (25 – 75 team members) running 5-10 individual Sprint Teams; to Enterprise level instances of (100 – 200+ team members) running 40+ Sprint Teams.

I've mostly implemented Scrum and specific XP practices as the most common Agile Methodology in my coaching and work experience. I've also been putting more and more emphasis on Lean Software _thinking_ over the past few years.

A Call to Arms

Finally, there are a number of impediments that stand in the way of Product Owners becoming Great—many of them are outside their control. I fully acknowledge this as well as the fact that the role is so broadly challenging.

My perspective in all of this is not to judge, but simply one of trying to _Raise the Bar_ for the Product Owner role—independent of their challenges or impediments. Their performance is crucial to a team's success and I feel that Product Owners, regardless of how conflicted, have a responsibility to their teams to step onto the path to becoming Great. This guide is intended to outline these characteristics of Greatness and set the expectation that every Product Owner needs to raise the breadth and depth of their performance.

If a single Product Owner cannot perform all of the functions that I'm outlining here, then it is his/her responsibility to put together a team that can meet these demands. To do anything less would risk reducing their and their team's agile performance to mere mediocrity.

So, become Great for yourself, your teams, your organization and so that you DELIVER on the promise of Agility!

Happy Sprinting!
Bob Galen
Cary, NC—Spring 2009

Chapter 2

'Role' of the Product Owner

I believe there are many schemes that can fill this role. One of my primary drivers for writing this guide was to illustrate the breadth of the Product Owner role to ensure that _someone_ fills in all of the various aspects. I think that's the crucial point.

I also believe the best Product Owners are individuals who fill the role and not some sort of loose committee that lacks consistent, integrated decision-making. We'll discuss this as an option later, but having it as a focus and your primary responsibility, contributes to team and personal clarity. I think this partially drives the tongue-in-cheek "Single Wring-able Neck" metaphor that Ken Schwaber introduced in illustrating the nature of the role.

There Can Be Only One?

As I sit writing this chapter in the fall of 2008, there have been some heated debates on the discussion groups and blogs regarding whether a single or group Product Owner best meets the team's needs. A response from Ken Schwaber stated that there is "Only ONE Product Owner". A part of me wonders if there's more to the story than that pronouncement. Surely, there are contexts where a single individual may not have the time or capability to perform all aspects of the role—particularly the broad role I allude to in the next chapter. What do you do in those cases? Not do it? Or, force a person to do something they are not capable of doing? I hope not.

I think the distinction here is, and perhaps Ken is saying this as well, is that there is a _single responsible person_ as the Product Owner for each Scrum team. Zero or more than one person is also not an option here as this one person needs to be ultimately responsible for decision-making from a business perspective.

Now that doesn't mean there can't be other individuals, who are engaged with, and helping the Product Owner with aspects where they are weak or lack the time to do a proper job. For example, as a Scrum Master I foster the idea that the team is responsible for the quality of the Backlog and not simply the Product Owner.

If important quality steps, for example refactoring critical components or repairing important bugs aren't on Backlog, then it's the team's responsibility to craft good Stories that represent that work. They, in some fashion, become the Product Owner for these specific, more technical Stories. They also craft the acceptance criteria and balance the effort for these stories against the more business focused Stories. They partner to create a more balanced and healthy Backlog.

I often jump in and help with Backlog grooming activity. In fact, I sometimes spend the majority of my time as a Scrum Master doing work that I think classically falls under the purview of the Product Owner. Why? It's because this is what is required for the team to get the job done. I also view it as part of the natural partnership between Scrum Master and Product Owner.

So, the key questions regarding the Product Owner coverage dynamics are —1) Are central activities being effectively covered? 2) Is there a single decision-making voice? If you have those answers, then to my way of thinking, much of the discussion melts away…

Always a Product Manager?

I see a strong trend in many organizations moving to Scrum where Marketing Product Managers are designated as Product Owners. That becomes the default assignment—even in cases where a single Product Owner can have multiple teams collaborating on shared or integrated code for a single product.

This can really overload the Product Owner. There are a couple of team roles that I've seen become quite powerful in supplementing the Product

Owner role. First, is the software testing or QA team member. They can provide tremendous assistance with refining User Stories and providing acceptance tests—focusing the team on these efforts. In fact, this is a healthy and common shift for most testers, moving their focus _up-stream_ to provide clarity and improve quality at the requirements level.

If you have Business Analysts within your organization, they too become partners in this requirements definition and refinement process. The Product Owner can't become too complacent and disengaged, but at the same time, having team members who are really skilled doing the work makes good sense.

I'd also like to make an argument that nearly anyone with connections to the true customer (or the customer themselves) can make a Great Product Owner. It really depends on your context and the needs of the team, with the key point being it doesn't always have to be the Product Manager. Certainly they will be part of the solution, but perhaps due to your business needs, they can play more of a backseat role to someone else with a different skill-set.

Conflicts with Product Management as a Profession

I've been in quite a few situations where I became frustrated with my Product Owners not taking adequate time with their teams. Until just recently, I thought it was mostly a choice they were making. Sure, they had a few outwardly focused tasks and needed to communicate with many types of customers, but certainly they had more time for their teams! I mean really, how much more was there for them to do?

Then I began studying the role of the Product Manager as it relates to the Product Owner. There's a wonderful group called _Pragmatic Marketing_[3] that offers training, consulting and guidance for the profession of Product Marketing, as well as, other aspects of more technical marketing. They've devised a model entitled the Pragmatic Marketing Framework that illustrates all of the aspects and activities of Marketing Product Management.

---

[3] www.pragmaticmarketing.com is an extremely well respected firm in this space. They've recently partnered with Luke Hohmann's firm Enthiosys (www.enthiosys.com) to increase their focus on Agile Product Ownership vs. Product Marketing and Management.

What's interesting is that the role of Product Owner only covers about 8-10 of the total 37 responsible areas of operation for the Product Management role. Many of these additional responsibility areas focus on company leadership driven areas, such as strategic product alignment. Imagine you're a Product Owner / Product Manager and you inform the CEO that you can't cover the strategic market analysis he needs for the board because your agile teams need you to work on the Backlog. Which one do you think should get your attention?

No wonder we have *tension* in the agile community where we have Product Owners who are struggling to balance their roles against organizational Product Management expectations.

I now have a newfound respect for the level of the Product Manager and Owner and, in most cases, recommend that they create a healthy, collaborative group to fill in all aspects of these roles as required. Because no good comes from a Great Product Owner who becomes a fired or burned-out Product Owner!

Additional Product Marketing Nuance

Rich Mironov, one of my early reviewers, works for Enthiosys, an agile marketing firm founded by Luke Hohmann. He actively partners with Pragmatic Marketing to improve Agile Marketing with their clients.

Rich, rightfully, took exception to my "in-the-moment" start-up assumption for the Product Owner role. He reminded me that getting the product well defined in the beginning is central to a successful project or product development; he wanted to ensure that I made this point early on. I absolutely agree with him!

If my focus for this book was broader, I'd gladly speak on such issues and challenges. But, that's not my focus. In order to include a bit more focus on his sage advice, I thought I'd include a few snippets below. Please read them carefully. Rich is 100% right in his council and you should carefully consider his points—

Role Clarity

Yes, a Product Owner IS part Product Manager. If you don't have a full-time Product Manager assigned and you ship products to customers for revenue, you will need someone to cover the entire product management role. That's typically a long to-do list which includes segmentation, pricing, packaging, messaging, benefits/features, coordinating with Marketing / Sales / Training / Support, etc. Immediately ask for needed resources. Either you can do this or, perhaps, a junior Product Manager who will work with or for the Product Owner.

You may be assuming that a Product Manager is already assigned and has helped set up the group. In which case, you'll need to decide which PM-like things the Product Owner will do, and which things the Product Manager will do. In my experience, the Product Manager performs all of the Product Owner's role responsibilities along with several others. That's quite different from the Product Owner learning to be a part-time PM on the job.

By skipping this bit of organization, or assuming the Product Owner can simply "do it all", gets the project off on completely the wrong foot.

Importance of Strategy

You're begging the question of where business value comes from, and who frames the problem. In my honest opinion, most Product Owners have no training or experience with pricing, packaging or actual revenue value (hard dollars); they use vague hand-waving to decide what they think is valuable. Again, a technically astute and trained Product Manager (having spent time talking to customers every week), will have a well-tuned idea of what customers will pay for and what would be an unpaid requirement for the product.

It's also important to have a company-wide strategy and a division-level product strategy. Product Owners need to understand how their products fit into the overall story, as well as, drive value for the overall company. This usually has only a partial alignment with product-level options. Product Owners, who prioritize only for their individual products, can miss half of the overall value and, therefore, miss all of the opportunities to leverage the rest of their company.

To sum up: It is not practical (or smart or effective) to have the Scrum Development Team work on a revenue product and then try to discover market facts while also building software. Instead, your company-wide and division-wide strategies are critical to understanding business value(s). A Product Owner who doesn't start here will often mislead the team and over-value product-specific features versus company needs, fit, architecture, standards, EOL planning, etc.

Nor is it practical to drive business value and feature selection decisions solely from reactions from a small set of customers and/or stakeholders at periodic Sprint Reviews. It's simply not a wide enough data set to make good market decisions.

—Rich Mironov

Rich nicely makes the point that the Product Owner role is a broad one and that Product Marketing plays a key role in quantifying and qualifying your projects before injecting them into a Scrum team. I think both points play well throughout the book.

A Clearly Defined Role

Many organizations are also making a huge mistake when it comes to staffing the Product Owner role. In some cases, they overload Product Owners with many teams and force them into a part-time role. In others, they ask the team to figure it out on their own, or assign a Product Owner that doesn't have the requisite skills to be successful. These organizations need to realize that skilled Product Owners are a full-time and critical component of their agile adoption strategies' success. That lessening their investment or trivializing the role is a quick path to failure.

The Product Owner role also needs better definition. It's superficially defined in Scrum literature and, you're pretty much on your own, to figure out the subtleties of the role. This short guide is intended to define what, I think, are the critical requirements (skills, capabilities, strengths, and patterns) of a Great Product Owner. It is intended to provide some "depth" to the role and drive the thinking process when Product Owners are being hired into, or staffed within, agile teams.

The point is—it's the most difficult job within the Scrum team and needs to be taken seriously…staffed with highly skilled individuals who understand the nuance of the role. Individuals who are enabled by the organization to take the time necessary to fully engage their role in, and deliver for, their teams. In order for Scrum and its associated teams to perform up to their true promise, we need to find and develop Great Product Owners for these teams. Essentially the rest of the book explores the many dimensions and skills within the role…

Trusted and Empowered?

One of the core tenants of Lean and the Agile Methods is the notion of self-directed teams. This implies, amongst other things, that you have hired good people with the skills <u>and</u> experience you need to get the job done. Therefore, as an organization and leadership team, you must trust them to do their jobs and not micro-manage them. In fact, instead of the team serving you, leadership should be consistently looking to adopt a Servant Leadership model and drive performance by serving the team.

Of course, you <u>do</u> provide direction and guidance; however, it is more so at the vision and goal-setting levels. Once you provide clear direction, stay out of their way and support their journey towards achieving those goals.

Specifically, that is at an agile team level. Beyond the team, it is extremely important for the organization to trust their Product Owner's abilities, skills, and enable them to make decisions and drive their products. This story or concern shared by one of my early reviewers, brings this point home—

As I read this section, I was reminded of a recent problem I've seen with Product Owners that I hope you will address. One of the most common complaints I've been hearing lately from scrum teams, is problems with Product Owners not being able to make decisions quickly enough. It seems they feel as if they have to check with others before making even the most trivial of decisions.

This is usually attributed to executive management not providing them with the ultimate authority to do so; they feel like they need to get approval before they can make any decision. In fact, I've recommended that one of my clients not pursue their agile adoption at that time because of this predicament. It obviously causes issues with prioritization and timely completion of work when questions cannot be answered immediately.

This is probably a common issue at other organizations and I hope you can address what a Product Owner should/might do in situations where they don't feel they have been given enough authority to fully implement the role. Some possible approaches as I see them include—

1) *Ask forgiveness, not permission – make the decision then let executives find out later (you need a lot of courage for this one);*
2) *Have Scrum Master intervene with executives to ensure authority is given (especially useful if Scrum Master is an outside consultant);*
3) *Educate and/or train executives to learn why authority for Product Owner is so important.*

—Shaun Bradshaw

Shaun hits the mark here on a very common problem in many early adoption agile teams. The organization is accustomed to command-and-control style management tactics which can totally undermine the effectiveness and impact of agility. Nowhere is this more destructive than in the role of the Product Owner.

His ideas for approaching the problem are relatively sound too. I personally lean towards 2 or 3 as the better approaches. I'd also ask myself if there is something being hidden from the Product Owner causing this behavior. For example: Is the team not transparent enough to senior leadership? Or, is there some critical project business driver or priority that is causing the behavior? Or, is it simply a lack of confidence in the Product Owner?

Getting to "root cause" behind your stakeholders' behavior can often be helpful in sorting through next steps.

Remember

With all respect, I think Ken Schwaber is wrong or too purist in his thinking about having "Only 1" Product Owner for all contexts.

While having a single Product Owner who has the time and skill to perform all aspects of the position is ideal, real-world dynamics don't always allow for that.

In lieu of a full-time PO, ensuring that there is a single, decision maker and distributed coverage of <u>all aspects</u> of the role throughout the broader team—can be a very effective alternative. Point is—don't get stuck in purist thinking. Use common sense and collaboration to get the job done.

And when you're scaling the Product Owner organization, think of it in broad terms when establishing skills and responsibilities.

Chapter 3
Basics of the Role

First, I want to establish that the Great Product Owner is a member of the team. Not all of the agile pundits would agree with this view, as the role is somewhat specialized and unique. However, setting the stage that your primary customer is your team and that you need to respond to them first, will set the stage for the *thinking model* of a Great Product Owner.

They are not on the sidelines of the team—feeding it requirements and judging their output. Nor, are they presenting team results to stakeholders in a project management or reporting capacity. Instead, they are a distinct member of the team in which overall success (or failure) is a joint endeavor. They've got some *skin in the game*!

This partnership also creates a more firm relationship between the Product Owner and team that enhances their collaboration and results. The team connects to the Product Owner and endeavors to deliver business value not only for the business, but because they believe in, and fully support their *customer(s) and teammate(s)*.

Ken Schwaber, one of the co-creators of Scrum, defines the role of the Product Owner as the "Single Wring-able Neck". What he's implying is that the Product Owner is a critical role to gain Scrum success—arguably, the most important role. Secondly, that the role is part of the team; if the team "goes down", so should the Product Owner. Conversely, if the team wins, so should the Product Owner. They are inextricably linked.

Beyond the importance of the role, it's also a leadership role. Scrum is setup, as are all of the Agile Methodologies, so that the *customer drives* the team's focus. In this case, the Product Owner is synonymous with the customer and this brings with it tremendous leadership responsibility!

The third point I feel Schwaber is making, is that the team depends on the Product Owner to give them the "*right" things to do*. They expect that you're working diligently with customers and stakeholders to quantify and qualify the feature set that will bring the greatest value to the business and value for the team's efforts.

I've worked with some Product Owners who felt that they completely understood their markets and drove their teams down a path towards project / product delivery. They did little in advanced qualification of the work or showing their customers early Sprint Reviews to gain feedback. From their perspective, why ask when you *know* what the customers need.

However, when the projects were finally vetted with real clients, we received the traditional feedback that frightens most Waterfall projects — "This isn't what we asked for." Or, "This is useless, we don't work this way". One of the greatest responsibilities of a Great Product Owner is to ensure that they've done everything possible to qualify the work their teams are delivering. Ensuring that it meets customer and business needs, not by perception or assumption, but by listening to customers, having frequent demonstrations, while encouraging plenty of feedback!

A Breadth of Experience

Another basic view is directed towards the breadth of the role. We'll get into details later, but I want to explore this early on. The Product Owner in my mind is:

- **Part Product Manager:** Deeply and broadly understanding the business needs for their particular product(s). Talking to customers (a lot!) and gathering information about their wants and needs. Communicating outward regarding team, product, and project "state" to customers and stakeholders. Creating a shared vision for where the market is going and how to leverage that opportunity. Translating that vision into the features and dynamics for a product and mapping it into "chunks or themes" for release.

- **Part Project Manager:** This is more from a forward thinking Product Roadmap perspective. They help guide work iteration tempo as it relates to the forecast vs. team velocity and release schedule. Often accomplished by building a plan towards market release timing which include product quality goals and testing, documentation, support training, sales training, marketing preparation, operations and deployment needs, etc. Creating a series steps leading to a sound release point.

- **Part Leader**: Serving as a focal point within the team. Motivating team members by providing compelling goals and objectives. Being able to make hard choices on priority and business value. Guiding and listening to the team in finding creative ways to _deliver more value with less scope and effort_. Defending their team and removing relevant impediments. Coming to understand what their team's strengths are and leveraging them to advantage in project workflow.

- **Part Business Analyst**: This is the requirement writing aspect of the role, defining artifacts (Use Cases, User Stories, or Requirements) for the team to carry out. Often defining acceptance tests and measurements for Done-Ness. A good part of this is to foster collaboration between architects, developers, testers, and themselves.

I believe this is why the role is so difficult to staff with a single individual and why the business minimizes it so often…the skill requirements are very broad and intimidating. I also think this is why a cobbled-together Product Owner approach is instantiated in many teams, as no single individual can provide the requisite breadth in skill.

Earlier, I may have implied that the cobbled-together Product Owner, i.e., multiple team members who assume aspects of the role, might be a bad idea. I actually think it can be a healthy alternative as long as ALL aspects of the role are covered and a single person assumes the "Primary" Product Ownership role—so, there is only one accountable Product Owner without any contention or external confusion.

Essence of the Role

Finally, the basic focus of the Product Owner within the team is Product Backlog generation and coordination. This is realized by first creating a Backlog and then, during the course of project events, changing the priority and flow to reflect the team and customer's needs for the product or project. An important part of this is defining Sprint and Release Goals that drive the team forward—by presenting a compelling, higher level vision for the construction timing and basic customer needs for the project.

This simple view is the _essence_ of the role of the Product Owner, which may lead to creating an overly simplistic view to the work. I actually find that many Product Owners fall into the trap that managing the Backlog is _all_ they have to do—which undermines the complexity and nuance of the role.

A Challenge and Ability to "Shift Gears" Story

Another one of my early reviewers shared with me the following story that highlights his personal observations and challenges related to the variability in the role of Product Owner. I thought it might be good to share it now in this section to illustrate another person's view to critical success factors regarding the Product Owner roles focus—

I think that the challenges of shifting gears between road maps and backlogs and internal stakeholders versus external stakeholders, are among the toughest ones - at least for me. Many Product Managers I have seen come from a pure marketing background and tend to have less affinity with engineering, sometimes resulting in challenged and limited communication. One of the trials I see, is that Product Managers in the role of Product Owners, are having to bridge between Product Backlog and Sprint Planning versus Product Marketing and Strategic Planning.

One is aimed at optimal performance while the other is aimed at predictability of annual deliveries. Marketing and executive teams want to know what will be released 12, or even 24, months from now and will actively plan market activities and revenue projections around those deliveries. Whereas the input from Scrum planning only provides us predictability for the near future, a successful Product Owner needs to manage expectations both ways and be able to shift between these two very different views. Shifting their focus without burdening one team too heavily with expectations of the other yet, always maintaining their transparency.

This becomes especially challenging when estimating Product Backlog items further down on the backlog. Often, it is really too early to get the team involved in any form of estimation. As you have stated, the CEO may ask you at some point if you are on track for a big release many sprints from today. Even if formal status is received through other channels in the organization, it is the Product Manager who is often associated with getting something done.

Additionally, while trying to maintain transparency, this can also have a few challenges. Some information might be very misleading to people further *removed from the process. For instance, I have seen some sprints that failed which actually increased my confidence of a team's ability to deliver simply because the time was right, the team was close, and I knew that failing a sprint is exactly what the team needed at that time to get better. Yet to outsiders, a failed sprint seems to sound negative or even alarming.*

—*Michael Faisst*

Remember

❖ Many people underestimate the required breadth of the Product Owner role which then lessens its effectiveness. Don't do that! Instead consider these 4 functional areas: Product Manager, Project Manager, Leader, Business Analyst as indicative of the roles breadth and skill challenges.

❖ While it IS about creating a Product Backlog for your team; don't fall into the trap of thinking that's ALL you do!

❖ As the story illustrated, the Product Owner role is a conflicted one. Partly focused towards your team, yet focused towards executives and important stakeholders as well. And let's not forget the customer in this. The expectation is that you're closely coupled to their needs and the value they seek. It's easy to be pulled in multiple directions so—being comfortable with that dynamic AND leveraging your entire team to help you is a key to overall success.

Chapter 4

A View of the Product Backlog

Great Product Owners essentially _own_ the Product Backlog. To quote one of my Product Owner friends, it's like "Table Stakes" for the role. They understand how important a well crafted Backlog is. They understand the nuance of now vs. later items and creating value and momentum. They understand how it maps to phased or iterative project delivery points. They fully understand that, while it is just a _simple list_, it's much more than that too.

It's important to define or, depending on your understanding of Scrum, re-define the nature of the Product Backlog. From my own perspective the Product Backlog is—

> "A Product Backlog is simply a prioritized list of work that the team needs to complete in order to deliver on the vision and promise of a product or project. It's composed of Product Backlog Items, or PBI's, which are succinct units of functionality or work, with priority implying delivery timing along with business and technical value."

For an alternate perspective, the _Scrum Alliance_[4] defines it this way—

> "The product backlog (or "backlog") is the requirements for a system, expressed as a prioritized list of product backlog items.

---

[4] www.scrumalliance.com – sort of the Scrum governing board, although it's primarily driven by Ken Schwaber.

These include both functional and non-functional[5] customer requirements, as well as technical team-generated requirements[6] "

Notice that I mention *all work*, as well as, feature and functionality items, which goes slightly beyond the Scrum Alliance definition. I'm somewhat a stickler for this…preferring to include ALL of the work within the Backlog. So, if it costs something to deliver it…I believe it needs to be *visible* on the Backlog!

For example, the following User Story—

Acquiring Performance Testing Software and Installing / Configuring it for Team Use …

…should be a PBI on your Backlog.

I would argue that it's more of a task than a feature, but it still belongs there. As does …

…Performing Regression Testing to Meet Regulatory Coverage Goal of 95% or
Meet With Operations Team to Plan and Script Release Deployment.

Product Backlog Items

In the purest sense of Scrum, as it was initially defined, the PBI's were simply entries in an Excel spreadsheet that defined requirements and/or work that needed to be completed by the team. Usually they were a simple statement of, at most, a sentence or two. There was little time spent defining the specific format of a PBI or, what constituted a *good* PBI, as that was

---

[5] Non-functional requirements cover non feature driven areas. They are often referred to as the ILITIES, in that examples include—Maintainability, Reliability, Usability, and Supportability. Quite often Security and Performance requirements are included as well.

[6] So here I could envision frameworks and architecture, refactoring or redesign recommendations, packages of bug fixes, and testing or infrastructural work as common examples of *other* work.

purely left to the implementer of Scrum to do this within their project team and business contexts.

Nonetheless, most early Scrum teams truly used spreadsheets for their Backlogs. The concept of a User Story then surfaced as a development practice within the XP (Extreme Programming) community. User Stories are requirement artifacts that are quite agile and lightweight; we'll explore them in more detail in Chapters 5 and 6. However, from my perspective, they've somewhat become the de facto standard for defining PBI's within Scrum and XP teams.

That doesn't mean that they're the only method. You can still have PBI's that connect to other requirement formats, i.e., Agile Use Cases or traditional requirement specification forms. Also, in some Scrum teams, the original 1-2 sentence guidance is still used as the sole requirement definition for the team.

For purposes of this guide, I'm going to focus on the User Story as the central representation of a Scrum PBI. I just don't want you to feel it's the only one. One of my main reasons for this focus is that the _behaviors_ surrounding a User Story represent solid agile practices and should be recreated around any other format you might be using for your agile requirements. So, even if you're not using Stories, you should find useful advice in these discussions.

For example, combined with the User Story is the notion of _acceptance tests_. These are verifiable statements that support the base behavior of the story. They contain your (the Product Owners) direction as to what aspects of the requirements are crucial; needing to be verified prior to your accepting the Story. Clearly, this notion can be applied to Agile Use Cases and any other form of agile requirement artifact.

Next, I want to share a short story related to prioritization. Sometimes we trivialize the effort it takes to truly create a well-ordered (Prioritized) Backlog. It can actually be quite challenging in practice...

Backlog Prioritization – A Story

I want to stress the <u>difficulty</u> of prioritization within Scrum teams. In my opinion, this is the most demanding aspect of an Agile Product Owner.

As Scrum Master, I attended a sprint planning meeting recently where all backlog items were marked "Priority 1". (I'm not kidding!) When I questioned the Product Owner about this, his answer was "Well, we need them all." He happened to be new to Scrum. I was disappointed that in my previous training he failed to grasp the important point that a Product Backlog needs to be clearly and uniquely prioritized.

I immediately postponed the Sprint Planning meeting due to un-prioritized backlog items. I then spent more time mentoring the Product Owner on how to prioritize and make necessary tradeoffs, to realize why this was important, and to understand the fact that prioritization is, in general, a <u>very difficult endeavor</u>. But, it does need to be done for the sake of the project. It takes a lot of <u>hard work and thought</u> to set priorities that are optimal to help the project become successful.

After this additional round of coaching, the rescheduled Sprint Planning meeting went a whole lot smoother.

—Mike Hall

The key point that Mike makes is that Backlog prioritization is really demanding. It takes effort, commitment and a lot of hard work. It also never stops. I hope that the back-story here is that Mike as the Scrum Master and his Product Owner used this as a springboard to their partnership and collaboration.

Another View to the Backlog

Another way I like to think of the Product Backlog is as a serial project plan or Gantt chart. I know this is contrary to a lot of agile pundit thinking, but it's true. The Product Backlog sequencing should have a significant connection to traditional software project workflows, for example:

- For complex or large projects, you should still be able to see some architecture definition and design phasing early within the Backlog workflow; clearly early on, and intermittently, as the design emerges.

- When leading up to a planned release, you should see testing maturity requirements leading toward the release; as well as, inclusion of other functional work (for example: documentation, training, operational readiness, and release steps).

- You should see riskier items being surfaced, developed, and tested earlier. In fact, risk mitigation becomes a central theme surrounding what you take on and when, within the Backlog workflow.

- If the team is unclear about major and minor work items, you should see references to research-oriented Sprints or User Stories (Research Spikes) interleaved throughout the Backlog.

- You should also see the team _actively_ contributing to refactoring items; testing automation items; defining architectural and design items; reworking of items, and getting together packages of meaningful, high-impact bug repairs, etc. within the Backlog.

The key point here is that there should be a great deal of execution nuance described within your Product Backlog—so, endeavor to view it in that way.

Alternative View – 2 Work Backlogs, 1 Workflow

I have seen other teams take on a different view to their Backlogs. Their experience implies that having the all the tasks -- technical, process, quality, and infrastructural work _mixed up with_ the product features, muddies the value focus of the Backlog. They actually prefer having two separate Product Backlogs.

One, as alluded to, is solely focused towards the feature set for their product or project. Everything on the list has clear business value and is a visible part of their application. The other list contains virtually everything else; for example—bug repairs, refactoring work, setting up team development or testing infrastructure, establishing testing frameworks, testing or process steps, and managing dependencies with other teams.

Their thinking surrounds _focus_. They, and their business stakeholders, are focused much more so on the _Feature-Based Backlog_, while the _Additional-Work Backlog_ is more in the realm of the entire team and much more focused towards the technical, quality, and delivery aspects for the application.

My major issue with this approach is losing the transparency of interrelated Backlog items and their dependencies and/or relationships. I prefer the idea of encouraging the "Business" to consider all work in an effort to remain _balanced_ in their decision-making. Clearly, in this scenario, they'll focus on the Feature-Based Backlog when selecting Sprint candidate work. However, you may run the risk of them getting a pass on the Additional-Work Backlog.

If you can truly influence your business stakeholders to balance between the two lists in determining the appropriate priority and workflow, then I think having multiple lists is fine. Then again, I've never personally witnessed this level of organizational maturity. Instead, the Feature-Based Backlog always seems to dominate the other work, which inevitably undermines the overall quality of the team's efforts. In spite of this, I don't want to discourage anyone from trying this approach to see if it works within your context.

Partitioning the Backlog

If any of you knew me, you would know I like to equate projects and methodologies towards the phasing within a chess match. I don't play a lot of chess, but I do understand the distinction between opening moves, middle game and end game and how they 'partition' the various phases of the game. You can similarly apply these same workflow characteristics to software projects. From a software perspective:

- **Opening Moves:** Are focused towards initial or setup steps in your project. For example, clarifying requirements, doing some iterative design, sorting out initial architecture, and/or planning refactoring needs as you move forward. Other start-up work such as forming or re-forming a team and gathering environments (tools, space, systems, etc.) are all opening move activities.

  Key focus: Emergent architecture and design, exploration, understanding and clarity.

- **Middle Game:** Is primarily focused towards construction of features and value for the project. In an agile context, this means delivering fully tested and delivered *packages or theme*s of features. It also means that ongoing refactoring and overall rework is being performed—as the design emerges.

  Key focus: Creating functional mass, quality, stability, maintaining simplicity, and delivering value.

- **End Game:** Is normally focused towards delivery. In an agile context, this means more traditional testing and general product maturation. It also means cross-functional readiness across the entire organization—everyone getting ready to deploy, support, and sell the new version of the product or application.

  Key focus: Stabilization testing, code freeze, quality, product integration, and deployment readiness.

I often get asked to assess the health and maturity of agile teams and projects. Since agile teams, in general, don't produce a tremendous number of artifacts, the Product Backlog becomes one of the core artifacts to review in order to gain insight into a team's agile practice maturity.

If I see a backlog that is simply a series of features, defined at the same level, I become concerned about the maturity and effectiveness of the team. You see I'm also looking for refactoring and design, quality, testing, infrastructural, architectural, maturation steps and release planning elements to exist in the Backlog. In these situations, I'll usually sit down with the Product Owner and begin to rework and refine their Backlog—establishing a broader base of the work to achieve their release goals.

If you're interested in seeing this concept in practice, you might want to skip ahead to Chapter 15 and the discussion of the Agile Release Train, which serves as a good example of the phasing I'm suggesting here.

Backlog 'Tension' Points

Related to Product Backlog composition, there are a few natural tension points within it that I want to explore next. How you maintain a balance between them significantly contributes to the health of your Backlog.

Level of Detail

PBI level of detail should never be the same front-to-back within the Product Backlog. Mike Cohn has written definitive books on User Stories and Agile Estimation and Planning; he speaks to this Backlog nature as being a pyramid or an iceberg. The items closest to execution, top of the pyramid, within the next Sprint have the greatest clarity and precision. As items move further out in time, down the pyramid, they lose this clarity. They also get 'larger' in size—he terms these "Epics" from a User Story perspective. They are placeholders for larger scale ideas that haven't been thoroughly broken down yet, nor vetted within the businesses' context.

This natural evolution of the Backlog supports the *Just–Enough* and *Just–in–Time* Lean thinking that we want in our requirements management and our planning.

Size – Does it Matter?

There is a good deal of debate over the size of the *typical* Product Backlog. From the Lean community, you'll hear a great deal of advice around keeping it short. There is good reason for this. As you move down within the Backlog, out in time if you will, one could argue that any investment in writing details down, and spending time substantially discussing Stories, is wasteful.

That *waste*[7] is from a Lean perspective where you don't want to invest much time in things that might change drastically and that don't provide immediate value to your customer. Instead it's much wiser to defer work to just the right time, and then doing just enough work to meet their (and your) needs.

There are other camps who think that having a list which represents all requirements for a particular product or project can be helpful. Mostly

---

[7] You'll also hear waste referred to as *Muda* in the Lean community.

because they feel it captures and illustrates the overall business expectations and scope. In this case, the thinking goes that you invest very little on the lower level items so, why not keep them around. They can provide insights to the team and stakeholders regarding overall vision, as well as longer term needs for the project. It also can have a sobering effect in that it influences scope reductions and adjustments by your stakeholders—simply as a reaction to the sheer size of the list.

I've seen both 'sides' work effectively, but lean (pun intended), towards the latter camp. I don't think it hurts to have an exhaustive Backlog, as long as you maintain your composure about investing in its development. I also believe you never know when items in the Backlog may spark some creative solution or stakeholder insight that can truly change the game. From my perspective, it's a fairly low investment, low fidelity mind-map that has a lot of visionary value for the team.

A potential negative side-effect of this approach is demoralizing your team, or your stakeholders for that matter, with the sheer perceived scope of the project. So, ensure that this isn't happening if you lean towards the latter approach. Here's a personal rule of thumb, or heuristic, for Backlog attention to details:

- **Short Term:** You'll need 3-4 Sprints worth of details in your Product Backlog leading to your next planned Project / Product release point. This is your short term vision for where you're going.

- **Mid Term:** Next is another 3-6 Sprints of mid to high level PBI's. Invest minimally in these items or stories. Size them roughly. Keep them short and simple. Perhaps cluster the items into packages or themes so that the team can better understand the direction they'll be heading.

- **Longer term:** Beyond this point, throw in whatever you've got on the list! Try to keep it in approximate, or rough, priority order. Invest ever so slightly in item clarity—better to have the items at a high level (Epics) throughout.

Another heuristic here is the 20/30/50 rule as *I 'heard' it expressed in the Scrum discussion groups*[8]. I think this is close to my view, but perhaps is a bit more succinct and useful view. It follows that—

Use the 20/30/50 rule. 20% proper stories ready to roll. 30% are epics - bigger stories that will eventually be split out into smaller fine grained ones (only as needed). The last 50% are themes - vague ideas about long term product direction and I never put much effort here because it's almost always wrong.

FutureCast

This is related to the sheer size of your Product Backlog, but I want to pull it out separately. Beyond items, work tasks, etc., I think the Product Backlog provides a glimpse into the future that is extremely important to represent.

First of all, it helps stakeholders to understand the potential overall scope of the project effort. Traditional or Waterfall stakeholders often fall into a typical trap of wanting a broad universe early on in projects—way before the cost or feasibility of construction or value is clear. This _wish list view_ to requirement lists that are never renegotiated is extremely unrealistic and not useful. However, it does fit into Waterfall's contract-driven way of thinking.

The Agile / Scrum Product Backlog model is much healthier. It implies that stakeholders can put virtually anything on the list—as long as there is a priority. As the team makes incremental progress, it becomes increasingly clear to ALL participants, including stakeholders, as to what the team's capacity (velocity) is relative to the size of the Backlog.

Additionally, as the team delivers incremental and high-value features, stakeholders realize incremental gains that change their views towards the remaining value of Backlog items. Having a large Backlog AND understanding the team's capacity in working through it (velocity of PBI's achievable per Sprint) can be a crucial step in managing these expectations towards more feasible goals.

Another part of future casting is bundling sets of Backlog features into customer release points. In my experience, release level planning is another

---

[8] I noticed this in an exchange authored by Mark Levison on November 12, 2008 in the Scrumdevelopment Yahoo Group.

of those weak points in many agile teams. They fall into a pattern of "Simple Iterative Release" where everything of value is derived Sprint-by-Sprint. There is no cumulative construction of product features that are deployed as larger collections. One by-product of this pattern is that the customer receives too frequent releases which dilutes the impact and increases their learning-to-value cost. It often fosters a scatter-shot approach within the agile team to deliver disparate features that don't connect well to solve the customer's challenges.

Hopefully, this discussion has, at least, transformed your thinking regarding the Product Backlog being a _simple list_. While it is—it also isn't. It requires thought, strategy, care and feeding, expansion/contraction—constant adjustment for you to effectively deliver value from your Scrum team.

Remember

❖ It's most important to keep the "tip" of your Backlog iceberg ready for execution. You do this by vetting—discussing, estimating, and refining the Stories, as well as including Acceptance Test definition, and improving the workflow of your team. This needs to be an iterative process or workflow that you schedule continuously with your teams during each Sprint.

❖ Effective Backlog management is about balance. Balance numbers, clarity / granularity, investment and value, and packaging. Each product / project team needs to achieve its own level—given its unique technical and business context.

❖ Remember the 20/30/50 rule and maintain appropriate "tension" in your Backlog. Don't be afraid to have a large list. It truly helps with scope understanding and negotiation. Just don't over-invest in the less important PBI's.

Chapter 5

Creating the Product Backlog

A Great Product Owner does not go it alone when they're creating an initial Product Backlog. In fact, they should engage their entire team in the process. Often _starting_ to create the Backlog can be quite intimidating. You simply don't know how, or where, to start. There's a technique that Mike Cohn introduces in his User Stories book that maps to running a _User Story Writing Workshop_ as a means of establishing a Product Backlog.

The idea has, at its roots, the same dynamics as JAD (Joint Application Development) workshops or similar requirements and planning techniques. These team-based collaborative approaches have been used effectively since well before the rise of the agile methodologies. Essentially, you invite your potential or current team in a room along with the set of _engaged stakeholders_ for your project effort. Get as many individuals, as you can, who will have a vested interest in the project or product outcomes.

Another important aspect is cross-functional attendance. For example, you'll want developers, testers, technical writers, trainers, support personnel, perhaps a sales person or two, and other Product Owners. You're trying to gain as broad a spectrum of functional coverage as possible to represent the various organizational connections to your project.

Even the developers can be difficult to engage because of their various functional areas. You'll want attendance from Business Analysts and Architects. If you have multiple tiers to your product development, then each tier needs representation—Web UI, Middleware, and Back-end Databases.

Setting the Stage

Probably the most important step in driving a successful Story Writing Workshop is preparation. While that's true of any collaborative meeting, where you want participants to produce artifacts, it's particularly important here.

Also, keep in mind that this is *your* meeting. You should be center stage— clearly providing the vision and setting clear goals; listening intently to your team, always getting them to focus on goals, while detecting adjustments that need to be made. Answering any and all questions; taking actions when you need more research, then ensuring follow-up. You're not simply using the teams and other stakeholders' time to create Stories for your Backlog. Instead, this is your first step at *crafting a powerful and clear direction for your team*.

Here are a few preparation steps that I recommend you think about when planning your workshops:

1. **Provide Requirement Vision**: The essence of a Story Writing Workshop is to produce a broad and deep set of User Stories (Requirements, Tasks, Steps, and Actions) that will encompass the product or project work to be completed—essentially, the Product Backlog. In order to get the desired breadth, you'll need to bring enough *character* to the meeting regarding the nature of the effort. I often find it useful to include others in communicating these points, such as key stakeholders and/or leaders from the business-side or architects from the technology-side.

2. **Define Key Goals:** Think of these as the compelling value propositions for the project. They should include not only key areas of customer value (1-2-3 focus points), but, also key dates or schedule targets, high value feature sets, quality targets, competitive pressure points, etc.

   Think of these first two points as relating to the *Project Charter* [9] for your efforts. You're trying to establish its reason for being and relay

---

[9] Traditional project chartering (from a PMI – Project Management Institute perspective) is something I think many new agile projects could use as a means of establishing a healthier starting context. It's particularly important as a means of connecting a project reality to stakeholder expectations. Most good Project

the value proposition. The intent here is generate some energy and focus by thoroughly exploring project details.

3. **Establish Meeting Structure and Organization:** As I mentioned earlier, care must be taken to get the *right* set of constituents together to maximize your results. This is a breadth vs. depth balancing act, but remember, this is your first stab at the Product Backlog, so you don't need to include *everyone* as they'll be plenty of opportunity for future contributions. I like to organize the meeting into several Phases as illustrated here:

   ❖ **Phase 1:** Introduction the Vision and Primary Goal(s). Also, cover primary requirements / feature sets of the Product or Project at a very high level. Usage scenarios are quite helpful here.

   ❖ **Phase 2:** Brainstorm the relevant User Roles that will help focus the User Stories in the workshop. This includes more natural user roles, as well as, system or external interface point roles.

   ❖ **Phase 3:** Of course the majority of the meeting is focused towards User Story brainstorming and development. In this case, for each role, dig down and brainstorm a set of Stories. Round-robin through all of the roles. Categorization, organization, and grouping into themes can be a natural outcome of this phase. I usually time-box the individual role brainstorming to about 5-10 minutes per role, including clarification of the Stories.

   ❖ **Phase 4**: Spend some time prioritizing an initial set of Themes and Stories for execution. You don't have to order the entire list at this point, but look for clear winners when it comes to Business Value and establishing early Technical Value.

Establish your own agenda around these or other phases and clearly allow for sufficient time for collaboration and discussion.

Management books have a solid discussion on aspects of Chartering. Appendix B also provides some brief guidance on project chartering.

Depending on the size of your project and team, the entire meeting should be time-boxed from about 2 to 8 hours. I will usually time-box each of the phases and prefer to be more aggressive with my times. I always find it easier to schedule another meeting rather than go on too long and exhaust your team's enthusiasm.

4. **Define Your Role:** Gather your thoughts around your own Product Ownership role within the meeting. Clearly, you need to be the one setting the stage for the outcome—since it <u>is</u> your product or project. But, what part will you play in fostering thinking around good stories? Or, answering questions? Or, capturing information?

    I've even found it useful for the Product Owner to occasionally <u>*seed*</u> the meeting with a set of Roles and High Level Stories that will serve to focus the meeting in broader terms. This usually gives the team something to feed off of and, normally, results in a better mix of Stories.

5. **Facilitation:** The success of the meeting depends, as much on the facilitator, as any other preparation aspect. Facilitation is an art and not everyone can perform it well. It requires some experience within the product and project organization and, at least, a superficial understanding of the problem space. However, the real key is finding someone who has facilitated collaborative meetings before, has *a tool-box of facilitative techniques* [10](yes, such things do exist), and an understanding of how to crisply move the team forward without losing valuable collaboration and ideas.

    Another suggestion is to find someone that can <u>*scribe*</u> the results of the meeting on-the-fly. This will help immensely in generating post-meeting momentum.

---

[10] Jean Tabaka's book (see references) is quite helpful here. As-is another book that isn't in the references—Great Meetings! – Great Results by Dee Kelsey and Pam Plumb is one of the best facilitative tools books that I've found.

Importance of Roles

As you approach a Story Writing Workshop, you have a decision to make. Do you dive in and simply start writing Stories or, do you try and provide some direction and structure to your story development via roles. I've found it incredibly useful to first brainstorm the key system roles and then develop your Stories within or under each role.

Think of roles in the sense of lightweight _Personas_ for actual users of the system you're about to develop—or, if you're familiar with Use Cases, as the _Primary Actors_ [11] within your system. The roles will cover physical users, for example—novice user, expert user, administrative user, non-English speaking user, etc., as well as, system-focused roles, for example—B2B systems, the diagnostic sub-system, the auto-update system, etc. All relevant systems, components, or interface points should be included. I've found that starting with a broad set of roles, then consolidating and organizing them into a subset of meaningful groups; improves the overall quality of your User Story writing by increasing the depth and breadth.

It also serves as a focusing mechanism. Instead of everyone writing stories from the perspective of the generic user, it gives everyone a much narrower focus on a per-role basis to engage their thinking. The key point here is, even if you don't think it warranted, always try to start your Story Writing workshop with role definition. It will make a huge _difference_[12]!

---

[11] I think there is solid synergy between Agile Use Cases and User Stories. One of the key areas is in the definition of Roles vs. Actors. I'd argue they are the same. In fact, the Use Case view of Secondary vs. Primary Actors might be useful within a Story context.

[12] Roles can also help align with Themes and Groupings when it comes to prioritizing your User Stories. For example, if you have a Legislative User role that is more important than other roles, then organizing along this boundary helps focus on that distinction.

Basic Deliverable or Outcomes

So, however you approach it, in the end I like to exit a Story Writing Workshop with the following outcomes and deliverables:

- An estimated 80% mix of relevant Stories for the project or product being surfaced and captured. Most are ill defined and epics, but a starting point.

- A very, very rough Backlog in sequencing or ordering. I think of the ordering in terms of thirds—that the top, middle, and bottom third of all the items are appropriately fitted in time.

- The top third should include the _Must Have's_. It's never too early to start sensitizing your stakeholders and team on what's truly important. There should also be some Themes in this section.

- Of crucial importance is coming out with follow-up actions; either planning for follow-up estimation, as well as, Release and/or Sprint Planning.

- If anyone had an initial, high level estimate for a Story, then certainly capture it. Otherwise, there are no estimates. These would begin to surface in the first Product Backlog grooming and estimation meetings, which we'll explore later in Chapter 8.

Figure 1 gives you a visualization of what your Backlog should look like existing your workshop—lots of stories, simple groupings, and time-based prioritization.

Caution

It's very common to exit the workshop with a very large and intimidating Backlog. Remember, you'll want to surface all of the work to contrast against one another and also to simply make it visible. However, product or project release planning will partition your Backlog into feature sets, customer release points, and manageable chunks of high-value functionality.

You will probably never get to all the work. That's more or less by design—driven by the Lean strategies within the methods. So, don't stress out over a large Backlog. Stay more focused towards the top of it along with your first and second release points. Time will always clarify the remainder!

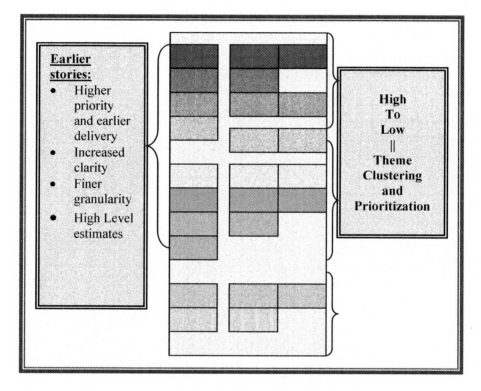

Figure1, Visual story outcome of Story Writing Workshop

Stories are a Practiced Skill

Even though User Stories are a highly accepted means for capturing Agile Requirements, there is still much confusion in the community surrounding their development. The confusion is exacerbated by two factors. First, there are not many available examples in the agile community—either on the internet or in books.

As I said, Mike Cohn has written the definitive text on the subject but, this too, is void of detailed examples of a User Story definition and hierarchy for a complex project. The other factor is driven by the very nature of agility. It is not an artifact driven methodology; instead, it is a conversation and collaboration-driven methodology. So, User Stories are intentionally brief and ambiguous.

The good news here, from a Story Writing perspective, is simply to _Dive In_ and start writing Stories for your application and business domain. Just do it! Don't get hung up on one versus two sentence structure, or completeness, or every Story needing the same length or phrasing. Just do your best, use common sense, trust your team, and just do it.

Over time, as everyone gains experience, you and your team will improve in your User Story writing skills. Your skill will naturally relate to your project, domain, and team because User Story structure and needs adapt to each team's specific context. Also, remember that with each Sprint, there is a Sprint Retrospective. Early on, you should naturally discuss User Story writing; estimation and planning improvements in your retrospectives as part of your natural inspect and adapt practices.

Remember

❖ User Stories, while not a panacea, are a wonderful way to capture requirements in your Product Backlog. Try using them. If you don't like User Stories, you always can use traditional requirement specifications or "Agile" Use Cases. Remember, the Backlog is simply a list of things to do—so don't get too hung up on format.

❖ Collaborate with your team and stakeholders when mining for requirements, ordering them, and planning workflow. Do this often as part of your general transparency—not only into the what, but also for the how and how hard of your Stories.

❖ Leverage roles as a means of driving a richer set of Stories. Remember that there are pure user-oriented roles and other, non-user roles such as API's, security risks, regulatory agencies, third party / contractual users, test applications, etc. Create a broad and rich set of roles, but don't create too many…3-8 is probably a good mix at the beginning.

❖ Practice writing your Stories! Effective story writing is a practiced skill and somewhat unique to the demands of each specific Scrum team. Be patient and work hard (as a team!) to gain experience in writing stories that guide _your_ application development efforts.

Chapter 6

Writing User Stories

Great Product Owners should have some skill surrounding User Story writing. They need to know what makes a good story—when it's too short or too long. They also have to buy into the *philosophy* behind the User Story artifact—where team collaboration and conversation is the most important element. That it's designed to be intentionally incomplete, which fosters much in the way of discussion and debate amongst the team members tasked with implementing it. Most importantly, its very use will place *positive pressure* on the Product Owner to engage with the team in discussing details towards implementing specifically what they want.

Three C's

As a starting point, it's useful to consider the 3 C's behind the User Story. The notion was defined by *Ron Jeffries* [13] as a heuristic to guide Story writing. The C's are:

1. **Card:** Represents the Story Card itself, either a 3x5 index card or Post-it Note that represents the User Story. Written on the card / note is the Story—simply one or two sentences that captures the requirement.

2. **Confirmation:** Represents the Acceptance Tests for the story. These compliment the story text and help to clarify what behavior the story needs to exhibit. It's the Card (Description), along with the

---

[13] Ron defined it as part of his XP work—www.xprogramming.com

Confirmation (Acceptance Tests), that provide the textual description for the feature or function being requested.

3. **Conversation:** Finally, and most importantly, there are the conversations that surround the story during its development. I usually envision a developer grabbing a Story card from the planning wall. The first thing he/she does is review the context of the Story within the technical landscape their developing in…just for a few minutes—thinking of design and construction steps.

    The very next thing they would do is _gather_ other developers, testers and the Product Owner to talk about the implementation from each of their unique perspectives. They craft a common view to the Story and the part each will play in implementation. They then go about developing the feature—pairing together whenever it makes sense. The goal is to collaboratively deliver the story without any later re-work…meaning it _meets_ the Product Owner's vision which is confirmed by the acceptance tests.

The most important C again, is conversation. To my thinking, the confirmation (acceptance tests) is next in importance and the card (requirement) itself is of least import.

What Ron is really trying to emphasize here is the third tenant of the Agile Manifesto—

"*Customer Collaboration over Contract Negotiation*". In this case I'd extend that to include *"Customer and Team Collaboration at All Costs"*.

The entire point to the User Story is not to get it perfectly defined or precise in advance. The Story is really a promise to have a conversation surrounding the work at the point of attack. It's this deferred clarity that is so powerful. You actually write Stories with intentional ambiguity—knowing that you'll resolve much of it during your team's Sprint collaboration and conversations.

As a Product Owner, this is the reason your Agile team needs you to be _available_. Not to ruin your day or waste your time, but to include *face-to-*

face communication[14] as your primary means of sharing market needs and context.

A Story Framework

Figure 2 represents a model framework for crafting the format of a solid or complete User Story. It first focuses on the user role, or persona, that the story is targeting. The next focus is on the behavior or functionality. The final point is the value proposition or what problem are we trying to solve.

> As a *<role>*
>
> I want *<system behavior>*
>
> So that I realize *<some business value>*
>
> **And can see that it does *<example>*

Figure 2, Story Writing Framework

A recent addition to the framework adds an example to the User Story. I think of this as mostly a usage scenario that can be executed to confirm the Story meets overall acceptance—so, it's a bit of an extension to the confirmation part, but it would be the most important confirmation.

Then on the back of the Card are detailed Acceptance Tests—the formal confirmation part of the Story. These are not intended to be exhaustive functional tests in the traditional Software Testing or Quality Assurance sense. Instead, they focus on the business logic tests that identify crucial aspects of the Story. Typically, there may be between 5 to 10 acceptance

---

[14] Why face-to-face communication? Studies have shown that our communication falls into 3 categories—words, tone, and body language. Across these, information is transferred at a 15%, 35% and 50% rates respectively. Clearly written documentation, while comfortable for many of us introverts, is the lowest bandwidth method, and while face-to-face is the richest and achieves 100% information transfer.

tests in the form of "Verify that..." or "Confirm that..." on the back of the User Story card.

As an example, the following story in *Figure 3* for a pet-sitting service, details a set of acceptance tests that provide additional functional descriptiveness for the developers and testers to more fully understand, and therefore implement, the Story.

> As a dog owner, I want to sign-up for a kennel reservation over Christmas so that I get a confirmed spot.

> ✓ Verify individual as a registered pet owner
> ✓ Verify that preferred members get 15% discount on basic service
> ✓ Verify that preferred members get 25% discount on extended services and reservation priority over other members
> ✓ Verify that past Christmas customers get reservation priority
> ✓ Verify that declines get email with discount coupon for future services

Figure 3, Story writing framework with examples of acceptance tests

Don't Go it Alone

Many Product Owners attack User Story development from the perspective that it's solely their responsibility to develop them. Nothing could be further from the truth. Instead view the development of these stories as a team function that only starts with the Story Writing Workshop; it does not end there.

Virtually anyone on the team can and should add or, much more importantly, refine stories within the Backlog. This goes for the story description and the acceptance tests. If you have traditional Business Analyst roles within your team, then they can certainly take on much of this work. If you don't, then your testers can adopt much of it. In fact, the development of a set of good acceptance tests is almost purely the realm of the testers on your team and they can help immensely here.

Story Characteristics

As you develop your stories, there's another heuristic to keep in mind that will help you develop a set of solid and properly framed User Stories. It's the INVEST acronym and it guides you towards stories that are:

1. **Independent:** As much as is possible, User Stories need to be developed so that they are independent of other Stories. This becomes important during prioritization for development. If every Story depends on another, then your Sprint Planning becomes nearly impossible to orchestrate.

2. **Negotiable:** You want them to be clear enough, from a business and value perspective, so that you, the team, and stakeholders can individually negotiate each Story.

3. **Valuable**: Related to negotiable, each Story should be prioritized in the order that it brings value (priority) to the business and customer. Each priority should be unique as well, so for example, every system backup feature can't all be first priority.

4. **Estimate-able:** One of the more important aspects of Backlog Stories is that their size is estimated so that the Product Owner understands the Level of Complexity and Level of Effort associated with each. The point here is that they should be relatively self-contained, with few dependencies, and _small_ in order to be sized effectively.

5. **Small**: Related to estimate-able, your Stories need to be correctly sized. First for proper estimation. But, not just for that. It also helps in, what I refer to as, Sprint Packing to have smaller Stories. One that can be completed by an individual or a small group within 2-3-5 days will assure that you can efficiently align work within your team.

6. <u>Testable</u>: Finally a focus on acceptance! Each story should be testable and acceptance tests need to clearly delineate conditions. For example, a tax calculation feature and all variant interest rate calculation boundaries, should be clearly defined as acceptance tests. In addition, all negative variants should also be defined.

When you're following INVEST in your story writing, don't get hung up on meeting each characteristic for every story. For example, you certainly will have dependent stories in most applications. The important point is to avoid, reduce, or contain them the majority of the time.

There are also some characteristics that, I believe, are non-negotiable— testable being one of those. As a rule, I expect ALL User Stories to have an appropriate number and level of acceptance tests that are *derived with and approved by* [15]the Product Owner prior to that Story making it to a Sprint.

Story Execution Readiness

We will discuss User Story prioritization in another chapter; however, I want to wrap-up this one up with the notion of readiness. Great Product Owners define 'Done' at many levels when operating within their roles. The lowest level is at the individual User Story. You need to ensure that your Stories are well written—short, clear, properly ambiguous, and with a full set of acceptance tests.

Foster an environment within the team where everyone collaborates on refining the Stories. The buck should stop with you when Stories approach a Sprint for execution. They need to be excellent in their definition along with pre-vetting (Backlog 'Grooming' will be discussed in Chapter 8) within the team. There's no worse feeling than having an ill-conceived and defined User Story hit the team in Sprint Planning that causes an hour or two of discussion and debate. I've been there and it's awful. Great Product Owners don't allow this to happen and it's here that we're going next.

---

[15] I know I'm being a stickler here, but it goes back to the Agile Manifesto point of valuing Working Software over writing about software.

Remember

❖ Use the User Story format as a guide—As a..., I want..., So that...helps to drive some consistency and quality in your story writing. At least at first until you get some solid experience across your teams.

❖ Communication can and will recover ill defined stories, so all 3 C's are important, but Communication rocks! I think of this in terms of when the Story is ready for execution—the team responsible for coding, testing, documenting and delivering the Story needs to "huddle up" and figure out how they'll be doing it. Asking the Product Owner questions and engaging them in the evolution of the Story through to interim 'acceptance' within the context of the current Sprint.

❖ Remember that the Product Owner doesn't have to write all of the User Stories. In fact, I think in healthy teams they perform very little beyond _seeding_ the initial lists and capturing User Story Workshop results. Leverage Business Analysts and Testers as _key partners_ in developing well defined User Stories. And the team as a whole plays a key role in it too...since it's really THEIR Backlog!

Chapter 7

Managing the Initial Product Backlog

Great Product Owners don't simply stop working on the Backlog after a Story Writing Workshop or after their first completed list. Indeed, their journey has just begun. In this section I want to share some tools for handling Backlog Item prioritization and estimation. You and your team will find them useful when you *Groom* your Backlogs during your Sprints.

Tools for Handling Priority

When I first read the Scrum books and began applying Scrum to my software projects, priority was something that appeared quite simple. The Product Owner was supposed to order the Product Backlog to reflect ongoing business priority (value) of the items on the Backlog. Nothing could be simpler—right?

Then, as my experience grew, I realized that things were not quite that easy. There was a lot of nuance in priority because it reflected the *workflow* for the project. That is, if *all* work for a project effort is on the Backlog (something I fervently believe), and the order implies execution workflow over time (which it does), then the Product Owner cannot make priority decisions in a vacuum solely through the working lens of "the business needs this feature now vs. later".

Priority has to be nuanced and considered against several other factors, for example:

1. **Business value**: For User Stories that represent features, then this is relatively clear. For tasks, research spikes, re-factoring work, training, bug fixes, etc. the distinction isn't quite so clear, but it's equally important. Therefore, business value needs to be *carefully weighed* [16] against a wide range of work.

2. **Time value**: If you view the Backlog as a representation of a project schedule, then timing of delivery truly matters. For example, if you should need to perform some work on testing infrastructure, then doing it too late in the release sequence simply devalues its impact on the project—just as deferring any critical bug fixes until the final Sprint is a poor strategy.

3. **Dependency value**: While we desire independence (the "I" in INVEST) as a prerequisite for good User Stories, the harsh reality is that there will be strong dependencies that come into play for meaningful execution. These will need to be accommodated as you plan for delivery. A good example of this is a set or theme of Stories that are customer committed to a release point. They will all need to be delivered together to realize the value.

   Another good example is to have multiple teams working on sets of Stories that have cross-team dependencies. Then the Stories would need to be integrated to realize their full value or potential.

4. **Technical value**: If you're collaborating effectively with your team, you realize that their opinions on technical flow are important. So, when you implement features from a development perspective considering architecture or infrastructural dependencies, ease of implementation, natural flow of implementation, ease of testing, and team member availability; all of which fundamentally matters from an efficiency and cohesion perspective. It also helps team morale if you listen to, and consider, their expertise and overall availability.

---

[16] This highlights one of the advantages to keeping business focused work versus other work in separate Backlogs as I discussed in Chapter 4—the partitioning can sometimes lead to clearer decision-making.

For factors 2-4, wise Product Owners truly engage in collaborative planning with their teams to surface, consider, and effectively prioritize in a truly nuanced fashion. Said differently, it's never a good idea to prioritize simply based on _Business Value_.

Group Based Prioritization

Now, I'm going to make a relatively strong recommendation. If you're working on a larger-scale project of any complexity, please prioritize at the group or theme level as much as possible.

Of course, you first prioritize (uniquely) every element in your Product Backlog (1..n). However, once you start truly debating priorities and sweating the details, take a lesson from how most agile projects plan and set your priorities at a level above the individual User Story. Work at the level of Groups of related Stories, or Themes of Stories that combine to deliver necessary and related value to the customer.

At this time, we'll examine two of the _simpler tools_ [17] that can be used for post Story writing grouping and prioritization…

Affinity Grouping – Themes

Affinity grouping is a very simple technique that is again, collaborative. Working with the stakeholders and team, place all your User Stories on the table. If you have a sufficient number of people, you can break into smaller sub-teams with subsets of Stories.

Each group turns over a Story card and briefly discusses what group or theme it might best be included with—creating group categories on-the-fly and freely moving Stories around dynamically—either on a table or on a wall. The idea is to look for natural affinity across the team as Stories _cluster_ where it makes the most sense to implement them.

As discussion and the grouping progresses, the team establishes a hierarchical set of groups that encompass the major components of the system or project being undertaken. This sets the stage for later prioritization at a group or theme level.

---

[17] I might sound like his spokesperson by now, but Mike Cohn has written the definitive book when it comes to agile prioritization techniques. I've chosen to illustrate some simple ones here. There are many more ideas in his Agile Estimation and Planning book. Check the reference section.

Priority Poker

Priority Poker is another fast technique that can be used to make a comparative distinction between Stories. It's not that useful for identifying individual priorities for large sets of User Stories, say for a 1000 of them. However, if you've packaged stories into themes, and have perhaps 10-50 to prioritize, then there is no faster way to derive a rough view to the ordering of those themes than Priority Poker.

Everyone gets a set of cards from 1...9, 1 representing the highest priority; 9, the lowest. A group of User Stories or Themes is selected and each discussed in turn. Not too much discussion though! Afterward, the team will throw their cards down with their priority calls. Members with high and low values quickly explain their thinking so you can optionally discuss, re-vote, and debate until you converge on a value that the group determines is valid. Then you move onto the next. A word of advice here is to let the voting drive the discussion—so vote often.

There are several variations on this technique that can prove valuable. The first one is placing some sort of limits or boundaries on priority levels. For example, limiting the number of priority 1 thru 3 Stories to about 20-30% of your entire Story portfolio or mix will make for some interesting discussions and/or debates. It also creates a more realistic and *varied curve* [18] in your Story priorities, i.e., influencing a trend so that not every Story will be a number 1.

Another variation is adding the notion of value. Each estimator receives a "pool of funds" to spread across the Backlog Story prioritization decision-making. For example, you might get an overall pool of $50,000 to spend on your Story 'votes'. A Priority 1 might cost you $5,000, while a Priority 5 might cost $500.

No bargaining is allowed and all/or nothing may be an option. As you're voting on priority, each number 1...9 has a specific cost that is paid after making that vote. Not only does this change your thinking and focus on value as it relates to priority, but it also forces you to make balanced decisions across the entire mix of User Stories and their priorities.

---

[18] I discussed the 20/30/50 Backlog focus relationship in Chapter 4, which supports this view.

There are certainly other ways to attack this, so be creative within your team. Also be selective, focusing on the *now* Stories versus future Stories that you might never get to.

High Level Estimates – Units?

There's a tremendous amount of discussion in the agile community around estimation of Backlog items. If you're using User Stories, then a common practice is to estimate them in Story Points.

If you're familiar with Function Points or Use Case Points, then Story Points are *not* the same. In the former cases, you actually try to size your application in these units (Points) so that they can be directly correlated to time—leading to effort cost and schedule planning. With Story Points, you actually try and stay away from this time conversion thinking.

Instead Story Points are a unit-less measure that tries to capture approximate size and complexity for each User Story. So, why is this useful you might ask?

Because when you're prioritizing your Product Backlog and ordering stories into themes, then relative size and complexity becomes a vital factor. In other words, 10 extremely complex Stories are not equal to 10 very trivial Stories. So, measuring 10 Stories as a team capacity or velocity, needs some sort of relative size and complexity weighting to make the velocity indicator meaningful across a *varied set* of Stories.

It also helps you and your team to plan out how many stories can be done in a Sprint by packaging up sets of Stories into themes. As you execute these themes, you get a sense for not how many Stories you can do, which varies considerably, but how many Story Points you can deliver per Sprint. This is a much steadier metric of your team's performance or output capacity (Velocity) Sprint over Sprint.

Finally, after you've executed a few Sprints, you can start measuring your team's velocity in Story Points—that is "We can deliver *about* 37 Story Points in a 2-week Sprint".

That knowledge can be extremely useful when doing Release Planning on your Product Backlog. Answering the inevitable question regarding—when will the *entire* project be complete? Story Point estimates give you a forecasting mechanism for determining your response to these and other questions while predicting more traditional project completion time-frames.

Two Level Agile Planning Abstraction

Remember, even though it might be tempting to convert your Story Points to represent time, try not to. It's important to keep in mind that it's a rough sizing, level of effort, complexity component, and not directly tied to time. If you do start tying it directly to time, your team will get anxious, start padding, fudging or manipulating their estimates. It's a more honest and valuable metric if you leave, or try as much as possible, to leave time out of it.

Remember, too, that Scrum and other agile methods maintain a *2 level planning abstraction* that I will illustrate below:

- **High Level Planning is performed at the Product Backlog level when:**
    - Stories and Story Points are captured and estimated
    - Release plans are forecast at the velocity level for sets of or Themes of Product Backlog Items or User Stories
    - Stakeholder commitments are *lightweight and variable*—as progress is made and your understanding of level of effort improves

- **Low Level Planning is done at the Sprint – Sprint Backlog level when:**
    - This is where Stories are broken down into tasks
    - Where the true effort for each Sprint is surfaced
    - Where true time emerges, less at an estimate level, more important at the actual outcomes reflecting the team's commitment
    - Connects to you're High Level plans—as the team works together, as they come to understand more, as their skill on this project increases…ALL estimates become more accurate (triangulate) over time

This implies that all Product Backlog / Product Owner driven planning is best kept at the higher level. While it is less detailed and ambiguous, it does abstract you and the team from diving to deeply into the details too quickly.

Planning Poker

There's a high level estimation technique that is quite popular in the agile and Scrum community called *Planning Poker*[19]. It is a derivative of the *Wideband Delphi*[20] technique where you gather together a team or group and perform a group-based estimation of User Stories or Features in your Product Backlog. Not only are you using the technique for estimation, but the more valuable part of it, is the collaboration and conversations it creates amongst various team members. It has the effect of fostering general understanding and surfacing implementation details of your User Stories.

Every estimator gets a small deck of cards that is loosely based on the Fibonacci sequence. The cards include— Infinity, 0, ½, 1, 2, 3, 5, 8, 13, 20, 40, and 100 which represent the Story Points representing the size and complexity of the Story. Similar to Priority Poker, when conducting a Planning Poker estimation meeting, the flow is along the following lines:

For each User Story:

1. The Product Owner or someone closest to understanding the nature of the Story explains it to the team…briefly for about 1-2 minutes.
2. The team gets a chance to ask clarifying questions of the Product Owner. I usually limit this to 5 minutes or 3-5 questions, so we don't try and over analyze the Story.
3. Then everyone throws a card (at the same time, not showing their cards early) that they think represents the size of the Story.
4. Then there is discussion surrounding the High and Low estimates. Why did you think it was so? What were your thoughts and experiences behind the estimate? Everyone listens and engages.
5. Next welcome additional clarifying questions?
6. The goal is to discuss, then throw cards again—until the team converges and agrees on their estimate.

---

[19] I believe Mike Cohn is the originator of the technique within the agile community. Certainly he has given it the broadest reference in his Agile Estimation and Planning book. He's also created a Planning Poker site that supports use of the technique for distributed teams, which is free and quite nice – http://www.planningpoker.com/

[20] Wideband Delphi predates Planning Poker. It was used in the 1980's by Barry Boehm and his Rand colleagues for traditional projects. At its core is collaborative (multi-opinion and conversation based) estimation, although with some skew towards Subject Matter Expertise (SME) contributors.

Remember, these are not explicit time estimates, nor commitments for doing the work. That will come later during Sprint Planning. Instead, these are _High Level Story Point_ estimates that should be used for ordering and planning the Product Backlog. As I've mentioned, they're of immense help when you're _packing_ Stories into Sprints and performing your Release Planning; they give you an approximate size and relative level of effort associated with each Story.

Another quick point is that they're _relative to each other_! For example, if you have a User Story that's been estimated at 3 Points, and one at 8 Points, then the latter is roughly 2 ½ times the size of the former—independent of the numbers associated with the Story Points. From a Product Owner's perspective, that's a valuable bit of information to know when making priority and value calls.

What are you estimating?

It's important to stress to the team that they're estimating _all_ work associated with each Story into a single Story Point value. Sometimes this is difficult and I've worked with teams that handled it differently, based on the types of work. For example, if your application is composed of Web, Middleware, and Backend Database tiers, then you might be tempted to capture 4 Story Point estimates for each Story. So, how do you then handle the scenario in _Figure 4_?

Story – Add new authentication and security checking logic to the B2B interface component	Story Points
Web tier	3
Middle / Business Logic – tier	3
Backend DB – tier	13
Testing	8

Figure 4, Example story layers estimate

Do you add up all the estimates and use that as the overall estimate? Or take the highest one as representative of the effort? What about the distinction between development versus testing work? Does this approach promote 'healthy' agile team behavior? Or does it foster functional silo thinking and a waterfall-esque, throw-it-over-the-wall mentality? What if, in this case, there was other external work by technical writers or operations groups. How would you handle those?

The estimating process can get quite complex as you try and align it against your group's functional skills structure. While I can see some contexts where this might be useful, I much prefer asking the team for a single estimate that represents the overall size and complexity of the work associated with each story—simply, _one estimate for all work_.

Not only does this make the estimation easier, but it focuses the entire team towards estimating the work to be done as a team versus the partitioned view that the above method fosters. This approach also has a tendency for the team to round up to the greater value. Since one of our greatest weaknesses as software teams is estimation in any capacity, this isn't necessarily a bad side-effect.

Remember

❖ For most Backlogs, bundle your User Stories into reasonable and relevant Groups or Themed packages for most of your prioritization and workflow planning. Filling in miscellaneous stories to "fill up" your sprints.

❖ Estimate all of your Stories, but emphasize that Story Points are High Level, Relative, and don't directly map to Time…so, don't spend too much time on them—throw an estimate and move on…as you can, and should, revisit them.

❖ The return from effective estimation is two-fold—insights into sizes for better Story decomposition, as well as, planning and collaboration around Story design and Sprint packaging.

❖ The Fibonacci series has the intentional side-effect of "rounding up" for higher levels of points. Not only does this indicate ambiguity, complexity and larger size; but it serves as a potential reminder for the need to break them down later on.

Chapter 8

'Grooming' the Product Backlog

I'm not sure I like the term, but 'grooming' does help make the point that a Product Backlog is not a static thing. Instead, it's quite _organic_ in nature. It _should_ grow and it _should_ contract. Not everything on it should receive the same investment of time. Things at the *top* should be quite granular and those at the *bottom*, merely a twinkle in someone's eye…usually coarsely grained and quite a large twinkle.

As you get work completed and items move up the Backlog, they need to be further examined and refined. Those refinements could include:

- Having the team reconsider them based on their priority movement
- Changing or reframing items as their original context may no longer be relevant
- Breaking them down further, splitting them up, and refining their estimates
- Having the team think about the prerequisites for each, the dependencies, and how best to package them into themes
- Simply generating more conversations and thinking around work that is getting closer and closer to execution

Grooming the Product Backlog is a term I've heard used to refer to this iterative and continuous process. As with any organism, you need to be caring and feeding your Backlog—and this is at a team level, meaning the entire team working off of a particular Backlog, should participate in its grooming. In this chapter we'll examine a few critical dynamics for keeping the beast well groomed, presentable and, more importantly, effective in driving each team's results.

Beyond Stories—Consider Themes

When you're grooming your Backlog, for the most part you're dealing with individual User Stories. However, depending on the size of your project and subsequently the size of your Backlog, it can be easy to get lost in the details.

An extension from the Story Writing Workshop, along with some prioritization techniques, is to deal with your Backlog in themes, or groupings of stories, that relate to specific functional requirements, roles, or sets of Stories that add more value together. This becomes even more important if you define finely grained User Stories, in that it simplifies important aspects of grooming—the time it takes for prioritization and overall release planning.

Themes have another benefit. They help to explain the overall workflow to business stakeholders and customers in terms that are more meaningful to them. You'll start discussing Sprint Reviews and Release plans within the context of your packaged themes.

Figure 5 is an example of the typical workflow that is generated thematically for an Agile project. It gives you a flavor for the workflow, and how themes need to be refocused and adjusted, as you approach each release point.

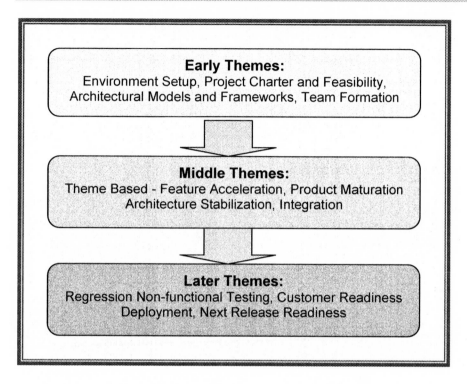

Figure 5, Typical workflow of themes leading to some sort of release point

Backlog—Themes—Time

Another characteristic of the Backlog, in my way of thinking, is that if you read it from top to bottom, higher priority to lower priority, and now to later you'll gain an understanding of the strategy that you and your team are suggesting for implementing the overall project or next product release point.

Now, of course, things become fuzzy the further out in time we go. Even in these cases, if you're planning on a Product Release in 3-4 Sprints, then the Backlog themes should change as you approach that event. For example, there might be Stories representing regression testing, or integration, or operational readiness training, or documentation and general sales training.

Now, let me caution you. This would be the flow when you're working in a context that doesn't release to production or the end-user every Sprint. If your model is doing this, then you'll see these mini-strategies within each Sprint's set of Stories. As you extend the Sprints that are building product or project value between actual releases, these strategies become more clearly visible throughout the Backlog. It really depends on how you and your team have decided to deliver value towards the business.

Grooming Dynamics

The ongoing discussions should continuously be focused towards qualifying your Story INVEST characteristics -- mostly by ensuring that they're of correct size, clarifying (or creating) the story and acceptance tests, and providing an initial estimate.

Inevitably, at least in all of my experience, the team will digress into design discussions as they ask questions surrounding each Story. This is quite helpful, as they're starting to align their thinking towards execution. You should foster this more and more as the Story approaches Sprint execution. But, only to such a degree that the team isn't being wasteful and/or getting hung up on too much detail…too soon.

Something I always remind teams of when they're grooming is the *Just-in-Time and Emergent* properties of agility. In the case of User Stories, we want to truly understand the nuance at the point of picking up the card and implementing it. That's when we need and will gain the true detail.

More importantly, the team is gaining more information about each Story as they get exposed to it again and again during each grooming session.

Idea Generation

I've seen some Great Product Owners vary the tempo of their grooming meetings or discussions so that there isn't the same focus all the time—that usually being, "Ask questions and then estimate this Story…"

They'll mix it up a bit. The first 15 minutes might be focused on introducing a few new Stories or, perhaps, eliciting new ideas for Stories from the team. This time is simply to chat about their viability and get an extremely high level estimate to help with initial prioritization and placement. Here they're also looking to generate brainstormed ideas for new ways to evolve the Backlog towards the overall project and/or product goals.

Next, they'll switch gears and talk about the Stories for the upcoming Sprint. Gathering the most important ones into a theme and then talking about the business drivers for it. They might open the floor to discuss relationships and dependencies for Stories within the theme. Is it the right set from a technical perspective? Can the entire theme be accomplished within the Sprint? Do we need further adjustments to the Stories? Breaking them up according to feasibility versus size versus overall theme needs becomes a point for discussion.

The meeting might then end with some requests for individuals to add acceptance tests for upcoming Stories and/or requests for additional technical Stories—bugs, refactoring opportunities, or Research Spikes.

This sort of round-robin approach to grooming the Backlog keeps the team engaged and active, as well as, keeping the Backlog fresh. It also sensitizes the team to the fact that grooming is a collaborative, iterative process that needs constant attention.

Group Grooming and Estimation Activity

There are several ways to perform Backlog grooming and none of them are mutually exclusive. Some teams set aside some time each Sprint, as well as, assign (via task cards) a little time for each team member to spend time grooming relevant Backlog items. Usually, the work is specific to a Story, or a set of Stories, that map to something in that person's background which make them a good candidate for the work.

Individual Refinement

This approach has the advantage of being less disruptive to the team at-large and reasonably aligns grooming with the natural workflow of the team Sprint-to-Sprint. One of the disadvantages to this approach, and it's a large one, is that it isn't collaborative—so everyone is off, more or less, working and refining individual Stories by themselves.

If you take this approach, you'll need a re-synch point before each Sprint where the team is exposed to Story conversations and feedback that has been going on individually. I've seen this take the form of a pre-Sprint planning and estimating meeting where the team is exposed to a set of Stories that are to be implemented in the next Sprint. It's similar to Sprint Planning, but since the at-large team hasn't had exposure to the upcoming Story set, it gives everyone the opportunity to gain familiarity.

Instead of the Product Owner being the only voice explaining each Story, the team members who vetted them are also quite active in these sessions— explaining their thinking on how they composed and broke them down, how they came to their estimates, their thinking surrounding design, and around acceptance tests.

The next approach is a variant of this meeting.

Group Refinement

Instead of asking individuals to groom the Backlog, this next approach is more collaborative and, thus, my favorite approach—although it does take a time investment across the team. Here, the Product Owner and Scrum Master schedule regular, periodic meetings during the course of each Sprint. I've seen them oscillate between one and two times a week, for about an hour, in most teams.

These are Grooming and Estimation meetings. The Product Backlog is the central focus for the meeting where the Product Owner usually projects it on a screen and traverses it dynamically throughout. I described my preferred format early on in this chapter under "Idea Generation" in which I explain that the Product Owner has several goals for the meeting agenda and keeps it lively by changing focus.

My experience shows that bi-weekly meetings are necessary when you're working on a new or actively evolving Backlog. For a mature Backlog, less frequent meetings are often the norm. Always keep in mind that you should try and re-visit each Story multiple times before execution.

A Combination

The reality is that I've used a combination of these two approaches to achieve the best results. Using collaborative meetings primarily, but also asking individuals to vet Stories in advance. Usually these are the more complex or challenging Stories. Ones where we need specific domain expertise or product experience to fully flush out options for the team to consider—thus saving overall elaboration and discussion time.

As a recommendation, I think there are usually about 20% of your Backlog items that need some sort of individual attention, outside of the Product Owner, before vetting them with the larger team.

Seeding the Backlog

One practice that I've seen work quite well is for the Product Owner to seed their Backlogs with data in order to drive improved collaboration and feedback. That is, when you're creating a new Backlog, or trying to foster further refinement, use your own ideas for Story descriptions, acceptance tests, and even estimates whenever possible. At times, I try and say something that's either wrong or outrageous just to get the team's attention to drive discussion and refinements.

My point here is that you don't need to bring every idea to your team 'fully cooked'. Rather, bring your ideas and use that as a starting point. I've found that this creates a much richer discussion than simply providing an empty or minimal list. At the same time, share your strategy with your team so they understand what you're doing and why.

Grooming also Drives Communication

A colleague of mine, Tony Brill, likes to remind me that one of the key roles of a Great Product Owner is driving communication across a broad range of interested parties. As is usually the case, he's right. The Backlog needs to become a central point, not only for the work, but for discussing all aspects of what needs to be done. It should draw customers, management, team members, other teams, and stakeholders into crisp discussion surrounding how to best accomplish your goals.

Given this, not all forms of Backlog items are conducive or effective in driving all kinds of communication. Sometimes you want to be involved with finely grained Story details, and at other times, it's more effective to deal with Epics. Tony has come up with a Product Owner communication matrix that maps to Backlog items in *Figure 6*. The bold items indicate the preferred Backlog item level for communication given the role and style of communication you're exploring. The important point here is to effectively adjust the granularity of your discussion as your audience varies.

Role	Exploring Opportunities	Suggesting Solutions	Facilitating Collaboration	Understanding the Marketplace
Customers	Epic / Theme	Epic / Theme		Epic / Theme
Management	Epic	Theme	Theme	Epic / Theme
Team members	Theme / Story	Theme / Story		Theme
Other teams	Story	Story	Story	Theme
Stakeholders	Theme	Story	Story	Theme

Figure 6, Product Owner – Backlog Communication Levels

Remember

❖ Groom your Backlog consistently at different levels—new stories, revisited stories, looking for themes, right before Sprint Planning, etc. Remember it's a dynamic list. I prefer a general rule that I revisit each User Story on the Backlog at least 3 times prior to executing it within a Sprint.

❖ Actively engage your team in the grooming process. Measure your success by the number of initiative based Backlog changes that the team introduces, as each team member should be adding, changing, decomposing, and removing Backlog items.

❖ Individual research is an important part of Backlog maturation. Engage specific Subject Matter Experts and other team members by using judicious Research Spikes to flush out the challenging bits. Also, there's no rule against team members doing a bit of "research" in addition to Spikes on the Backlog.

Chapter 9

Goal Setting at MANY Levels

One of my greatest frustrations in coaching many agile teams is their lack of focus on goal-setting. I see many Sprints that have weak and/or non-existent goals with the Product Owner coming into the planning meeting too focused on a set of stories or features, thus, *forgetting* about goal setting.

In my view, goal setting is one of the most important responsibilities of a Great Product Owner. It's how you set the stage for, and motivate your team. It's ultimately how you measure their success towards meeting your goals. Not simply by delivering some arbitrary number of User Stories or Themes, but driving them towards delivering high business value.

It's also how you drive creativity within your agile teams. How can the team solve real problems if they're simply following your lead and are measured by a list of features? I think the point is—they can't. I contend that self-directed teams need *vision setting goals* in order to drive their efforts, creativity, and ultimately their work. A key component of the Product Owner's role is to collaborate with their business partners and stakeholders determining their needs—then covert those needs into a compelling strategy and set of goals that guide their teams' forward progress!

A Goal Story

I was coaching a team in their first use of Scrum. It was a very small, entrepreneurial start-up company that was looking for an early round of funding. They planned on demonstrating their software at a prestigious Venture Capital conference where each start-up company received six minutes to present their product idea on stage. Since the conference was on a fixed date and they had historically struggled to hit their date targets, they wanted to try something new...Scrum. Given the circumstances and implications, I cautioned them against such a risky strategy, but they were adamant.

The Sprint Goal in this case, their very first one, was to—"Create a compelling demo and stir investment interest amongst the VC's at the event". That was it. The product was a SaaS[21] software process application with a myriad of process measurement functions. However, they had six minutes to put it through some interesting paces in order to illustrate its true potential.

Their newly minted Product Owner quickly put together a series of Stories that he thought were compelling and the team went and planned their first sprint.

Almost immediately these planned Stories were impacted by real feature limitations and bugs in the application. As a result, the Product Owner had to make many adjustments over the initial few days—changing and fine-tuning the Stories associated with the Sprint. Task assignments also frequently changed—in some cases including additions and deletions.

Long story short—they derived a compelling demo story during the sprint and won significant funding. Did the original stories and tasks remain constant? No. However, the Sprint Goal was the driving constant that they measured all changes against. In the end, the goal steered their adjustment focus and efforts and they met the goal.

---

[21] SaaS – Software as a Service deliver model. Think of it as a 'hosted' solution.

Charter – Vision and Mission

The first level of goal setting is at the overriding project or meta-release level. I usually think of this as traditional project chartering, but with an agile flavor. It's always worthwhile for the Product Owner to sit down with their business colleagues and key stakeholders to define an overall mission and vision. These are typically high level objectives, but ones in which you detail the _Prime Directive_ for the project or product development effort. Here's a quick example—

> _Our vision is for this release to substantially change the inventory management and check-out logic in our marketplace support to improve our customer experience._

> _Our mission is to fix the approximately 200+ bugs in this space, re-factor the checkout UI interfaces, and improve DB performance within Inventory by a factor of 5 times._

The key benefit in setting the Vision and Mission is that it laser focuses the team about what is important at a _release_ level, and should, hopefully, drive Story prioritization, Sprint Planning, and overall team execution.

Release Goals

Release goals are another step down from the overall Vision and Mission. This would be a major step towards realizing the overall vision. As we move down in granularity, it's important to make your goals as crisp as possible. There's an acronym that helps here that you've probably heard before called SMART…

SMART – Explained

When you're creating release criteria, consider how they measure up to the following—

<u>Specific</u> – This is the *"what and how"* behind the criteria— what you need to create and/or how should you support a requirement.

<u>Measurable</u> – Think in terms of tangibly measuring completion of the goal -- how will you know when it's been met?

<u>Attainable</u> – This is the *"how"* behind the goal. You need to be able to envision achieving it within the constraints and bounds of your project.

<u>Realistic</u> – Given the project constraints and team dynamics, the goal needs be do-able with appropriate planning and effort.

<u>Trackable or Time Bound</u> – The goal has a clear timeframe or target for completion.

Figure 7, SMART Acronym Explained

SMART should be a guiding model for all of your goals and criteria— making them as *smart* as possible. For our sample flow, then a release goal might have the following format:

Within the next 3 development sprints, prioritize and attack the highest priority 150 defects, releasing and verifying fixes after each Sprint. In addition, re-factor DB functionality within the Inventory Management Component so we can measure precise performance.

So, why define goals? What's the point? The answer is to measure your achievement relative to them. In this case, the team will be planning all of their work relative to the above goal. Of course, they will measure their tasks and features delivered—determining their velocity. This will give them a sense of their overall effort, their challenges, and their performance.

They should ultimately be measured against how they delivered against the _goal_. This is the one thing that should be _accomplished_, with everything else being simply a means to this end.

Sprint Goals

Every Sprint should have a goal and it shouldn't relate to getting specific stories done, or working hard, or making the business _happy_. Instead, each Sprint should have a compelling goal that is tied to the business and stakeholder needs. It should also align with the overall vision and mission and the release goals. Just to complete the exercise, here would be a reasonable Sprint goal for the example goal sequence:

> _In this Sprint we're going to resolve the Top 50 bugs that are located throughout the Inventory Loop-Up / Reconciliation Components and, then, resolve them. Particular attention will be paid to inconsistent data handling and adding future diagnostics for Inventory Performance monitoring._

I hope you connected the "drill down" nature of good goal setting and how they provide _cohesion_ for your efforts.

Done-Ness Criteria

I gave a talk at the 2008 Agile Conference and had the wonderful opportunity to walk around networking and learning for five whole days. One of my observations during the week was the number of presenters that emphasized _Done-Ness Criteria_ in their discussions. I'd say at least 5-8 presentations referred to them in various forms.

This aligned quite nicely with my own experience as it is absolutely critical to define multi-level goals within your agile teams. The final level of these goals should be _Done-Ness_, as done will need to be defined for each functional team role and for your features, in general, via acceptance tests.

At the functional level your developers, testers, and virtually all team members should decide the work practices and steps required to actually declare a piece of work to be completed. Let's pick on developers for a second; however, the point applies to all team members. If I've developed a component and want to declare it done within my current Sprint, we might want to check-off on the following:

Team alpha—Developer Done-Ness Criteria

✓ Code is complete
✓ Reviewed code w/component SME
✓ Code checked-in
✓ Build worked; resolved ALL build issues
✓ Unit tests were defined where appropriate; nothing less than 40% coverage
✓ Code contains FIT fixtures where appropriate for testing
✓ Collaborated with Tester on FitNesse test cases for feature acceptance
✓ Acceptance tests passed
✓ Partial Regression tests passed
✓ Demonstrated functionality to Product Owner—received interim "Thumbs Up"

Figure 8, Sample Done-Ness Criteria from a Development Perspective

Setting solid *Done-Ness* Criteria has several important benefits within your team:

- First, it helps with Sprint Planning and Estimating since each team member has a very clear idea as to what is expected of them in performing and completing their work.
- It also helps to reinforce consistency in deliverables—setting the expectations across the entire team for their quality.
- Another benefit, as you can see in the example, it serves to reinforce solid agile collaboration across the team.

Done-Ness is not typically driven solely by the Product Owner. It's more of a team initiative and agreement—along the lines of how to *professionally deliver* high quality software. However, the Product Owner clearly has a voice in the definition of, quality of, and breadth of *Done-Ness Criteria* across the team.

Why? Because it drives overall quality and the level has a very clear cost to the business. You have to understand, support, and be willing to pay for the costs of your Done-Ness criteria. From that perspective then, you're an important driving factor.

Release Criteria

Done-Ness also extends to the Release Level. In this case, I think of it as equivalent to old-fashioned Release Criteria, as most of us have experienced, in more traditional or Waterfall projects. Traditionally, Release Criteria spoke in terms of the specific requirements for achieving a release point. Factors that might be mentioned include:

- **Quality Criteria:** Focuses towards product or application quality levels that you're trying to achieve (test coverage and traceability targets, acceptable bug levels and actions, workaround guidelines, as well as, identifying the types of testing required).

- **Functional Criteria:** Illuminating the specific set of related features required to meet the customers' needs. Speaking of any tradeoffs or compromise and defining key success criteria).

- **Process Criteria:** Steps necessary to prepare the organization to properly deploy and support the customer with the release. This would include organizational and important software process checkpoints.

- **Performance Criteria:** Literally the performance characteristics the software must achieve (performance, minimal platform support levels, interoperability checks) prior to release.

Typically, these criteria would be established in the beginning of a project or product development effort—usually during requirement definition or chartering. They would align with key success criteria for the project and guide decisions along the way towards the release.

In an agile context, these criteria are less encompassing and perhaps more holistic than their Waterfall cousins. However, it is helpful to define a set of criteria for each release—learning from the traditional approaches to defining them. Don't be put off by these criteria simply because of their traditional flavor. I've found it extremely helpful to drive agile releases targets with release criteria; I suspect you will too.

Johanna Rothman and I have written *articles*[22] focused on release criteria. If you're interested in further refining yours, you might want to take a look.

---

[22] www.stickyminds.com is a repository for sets of materials by Johanna and me—more so from her though. If you have an SQE Powerpass, you can access all of the content. Here's a link to an early article that Johanna wrote on Release Criteria - http://www.stickyminds.com/getfile.asp?ot=XML&id=5889&fn=SmzXDD2224file listfilename1%2Epdf . You can also email me to request one I wrote for Better Software in 2006.

Remember

❖ Release Criteria are probably the broadest of any goals you will define because they're focused on the breadth of work and expectations surrounding customer delivery. Gather them from within your team, but also across your stakeholders and customers—the earlier the better.

❖ It is CRUCIAL to define clear Done-Ness criteria for team deliverables (Story Acceptance and individual engineer work products). In lieu of command-and-control checkpoints, these become the drivers for high quality software. Hold yourself and your team accountable to Done-Ness!

❖ For any "New" project or product effort, strongly consider developing a Project Charter and connecting all of your criteria to it. There are many definitions for it and I'd bet your organization has its own variant. What's important is to Charter; and not necessarily the format. Appendix B provides some chartering insights.

❖ With self-directed teams, the way to drive their behavior, focus, and performance is not by telling them what to do. It's by providing clear and consistent goals that compel them forward by showing the way.

❖ Goals are intended to be measured against. Be honest in your assessments of how you are meeting your goals. If you're not meeting them, then say that in your retrospectives and do something about it!

Chapter 10

Sprint Planning

Great Product Owners take the Sprint Planning meeting very seriously. They realize that, while agility isn't necessarily about planning, it is extremely important to start each Sprint properly! I've been part of some of the *ugliest* Sprint Planning meetings imaginable—ones where the Product Owner came in with a set of stories that hadn't been properly vetted with the team, or where the team hadn't participated in Backlog grooming—so they were totally unprepared for the meeting.

In all cases, the meetings took forever, were frustrating, sometimes needed to be cancelled and then rescheduled. It clearly set the wrong tone for the upcoming Sprint. In all cases, these issues could easily have been avoided by simple pre-meeting planning.

Typical Dynamics

The recommended dynamics for the length and focus of a normal Sprint Planning session seem to vary considerably; not only in books, but from team to team as well. The Schwaber 2001 Scrum book's recommendation is that Sprint Planning should allocate an entire day for a 30-day Sprint, 4 hours for Backlog and Sprint Goal reviews and 4 hours of Sprint Backlog planning time for the team.

I often refer to these as Part A and B of the meeting. *Part A* is the domain of the Product Owner. In it, you should focus on relaying the Sprint Goal(s) and describing the feature or Story set that you want to have implemented. This is not the time for changing your mind or focus. Instead, you should confidently present the contents, the business priority and value, and then, address any clarifying questions the team may have.

Once the team has a solid, high level understanding of where they're going, the meeting shifts to *Part B,* or Sprint Backlog (task) planning. While the Product owner is fully engaged in this part as well, the second half of the meeting is really for the team. It's where they perform task breakdowns for each Story, contemplating design and dependency details, and start fitting work across themselves for the Sprint.

Outcomes are an important measure for planning; the team should exit Sprint Planning with the following minimal set of artifacts and/or understandings:

- ✓ A Sprint Goal that is clear, measurable, compelling and one that everyone understands & supports.
- ✓ A set of committed Product Backlog Items or Stories that align with the Sprint goal(s).
- ✓ Every team member has time clearly committed to the Sprint (preferably at 100% of their individual capacity, but minimally with a declared capacity).
- ✓ A set of tasks associated with each Story estimated at a relatively fine level of granularity.
- ✓ Work clearly identified for each team member for, at least, the first day of the Sprint.

A Diversion – Task Granularity

One of the major variations in many agile teams is how they attack Sprint or iteration planning. I prefer that tasks are broken down into hours, but not too finely grained—so no smaller than 4 hours and no larger than 2-3 days on average. I've seen other ends of this spectrum used as well—sometimes working and more often not.

Estimating in 1-4 hour increments for tasks seems to create a false sense of comfort and understanding. Often this is the case because it is too finely grained and takes forever to finish planning while operating at this extreme level of granularity. Estimating in units of 3-5+ days implies too coarse a level of granularity and prevents appropriate team visibility in getting the work done. Also, it often introduces risk because team members aren't completing tasks quickly enough—moving them to a "Done" state. It can lead to *90% done syndrome* where nothing, or very little, actually gets completed by Sprints' end.

As I've said, I prefer the guideline of tasking being in the 4 hour to 2-3 day range. This seems to give the right balance in planning visibility without micro-managing the work.

Another Diversion – The 'Point' of Sprint Planning

I'm going to state something that may be contrary to your experience or counterintuitive, but my experience holds it to be true. The tasks defined in Sprint Planning really don't matter a great deal. Instead, they're simply a means to an end. What really matters is that the team has a *Goal* and signs-up to meet it by delivering a set of User Stories or features that support it. That is the *Prime Directive* for each and every Sprint.

At some level, it doesn't matter how many tasks there are, nor their estimates for effort, or who has, or has not, signed up for them. Sure, having elicited them has some value from the perspective of giving the team an initial road-map for the Sprint. But, what if they need many adjustments to achieve the Sprint goal? Do we throw out the goal because of the change in game plan? Of course not!

The crucial point here is related to focus. Should the team simply focus at a task level, getting them individually done or, should they focus all their energy towards the goal. I've had much improved delivery performance when we've focused towards the latter.

So the point of Sprint Planning is:

1. To share and gain the team's commitment toward the Sprint Goal
2. To identify the set of User Stories that align with and are feasible to deliver within the Sprint.
3. To identify the tasks associated with delivering those User Stories.

Clearly, in that priority order and leading to *goal-driven work*.

Sprint Planning Adjustments

I often find that Sprint Planning time can be exaggerated and that optimizations are possible without compromising the quality of the meeting. A couple of points come to mind when making adjustments to your Sprint Planning meetings—

Shorter Sprints and Meetings

I prefer shorter, more focused planning sessions. Part of the dynamics surrounding this is to have shortened Sprint lengths and smaller teams. I try to keep most sprints to about 2 weeks in length and think optimum team size is 5 +/-2, instead of the 7 +/- 2 recommended by Ken Schwaber in his 2001 Scrum book. Therefore, if you have smaller iterations and teams, you should be able to shorten the meetings significantly.

The other dynamic is your preparation. I'm convinced, because I've seen it done so often, that you can conduct a complete Sprint Planning meeting (*Parts A and B*) in 2-3 hours for a 2-week Sprint, _IF_ you've properly vetted the Backlog and have a small, focused team.

Taking Too Long

If your team finds itself spinning their wheels in a Sprint Planning meeting, as the Product Owner you should take primary responsibility for it. Clearly, the team isn't familiar enough with or prepared to do the work. Rather than sitting around and debating approaches and feature nuances, it's probably more congruent to cancel the meeting to figure out the appropriate next steps offline.

That same logic applies if you simply exceed your time-box for the meeting. Check in with your team and Scrum Master at this point. I've, at times, run a mini-retrospective with the team to determine where we lost our planning focus and to discuss how to get things back on track.

Distributed Sprint Planning

In some cases, you may have a distributed Scrum team working on your Backlog. This can be an effective relationship if you spend time to include the team in all Backlog vetting and collaboration surrounding Backlog preparation.

There are certain Scrum activities that I feel all team members need to participate in regardless of locale. Sprint Planning is one of those activities. No matter how challenging or difficult, remote team members need to be included in the meeting. I've seen tools like web cams, wiki's, and skype to be useful in pulling teams together. There are also mature, enterprise-level agile tools that can be of immense help in these scenarios.

Distributed Team Story

I encountered a team that was virtually split across two sites— one in Richmond, Virginia; the other, in Atlanta, Georgia. Fortunately, both teams were in the same time zone making working together that much easier.

They had experimented with a variety of ways to <u>connect</u> the two sites effectively for agile collaboration. When I happened upon them as a coach, they had settled on the following:

They setup two planning boards in both locales that represented their plans and progress for each Sprint. They had also setup a webcam in each location. Each webcam was fixed on the planning boards and team areas so each group could see what was happening on the "other side".

In addition, they chose to keep a conference call line open—initially, just for meetings (daily scrum planning, estimation, reviews, etc.); later on, all of the time. The reason they shared for this was that it created a <u>tighter coupling</u> between the groups in that each could continuously hear conversations from the other location.

They spoke of gaining the ability to <u>sense</u> when a remote discussion affected someone locally, and simply turning their attention to the phone to join the discussion. This gave them the feeling of physically being together, by being able to overhear and engage in appropriate discussions.

During Sprint Planning, each side took ownership of posting ALL cards on their respective planning walls. It happened quite naturally and every team member participated in asking questions, writing, and posting. Again, it "felt" like a single team.

I found the simplicity and effectiveness of the team's solution to be quite remarkable.

Meeting Preparation

It starts with a properly prepared Product Backlog that contains sufficient clarity around the Product Backlog Items or User Stories that may come into play in the Sprint. I have a personal guideline to vet stories with the team at least 3 times before they're exposed to them in the Sprint Planning meeting.

Why?

To allow them time to provide estimation information, to suggest different feature decomposition boundaries, to have the team begin thinking of dependencies and design approaches and, in general, just to become more comfortable with each Story and overall *theme* of the Sprint.

The first exposure point is in a Story Writing Workshop is first created within the project and team. The second point is in a Product Backlog grooming meeting where I will re-visit the Story to freshen the definition with the team. This usually occurs about 1-2 Sprints before I think it will be picked up for construction.

The final point is the week before the next Sprint, in the Product Backlog grooming meeting. I prefer to do a final quick review of the upcoming contents. Much of the focus is on the team's readiness for these Stories and sorting out whether they've worked off-line to understand and anticipate the work. If I get a lot of blank looks or tons of questions, it means that the team isn't prepared for the Sprint and we'll need more focused time to get prepared.

Vetting Alternative – Technical Planning Meeting

At times, the team may need additional time to familiarize themselves with a set of features to be implemented in the next Sprint. This is beyond the venue of their normal Backlog grooming and estimation meetings. I've found this is usually needed in teams where you have complex or specialized domain-centric work coming up that the team, as a whole, isn't generally familiar with. Often this happens in larger-scale projects or when there are many new team members.

The session allows the entire team to spend time on "pre-preparation" for the Sprint fostering higher level design discussions, Q&A, and simple game planning for the upcoming work. More than likely, the Scrum Master and Product Owner won't attend. They'll simply kick-off the meeting and then leave. It's really the team's meeting; so, consider it a sort of group based design or code review, but at a Story level.

Normally, I'll time-box the meeting to 1-2 hours and schedule it a day or two before the Sprint Planning session. While I acknowledge that it's a little wasteful from a Lean perspective, it can be a very powerful event by allowing the team to sort through global dependencies for a Sprint's worth of work at the same time as brainstorming the best plan-of-attack.

In some contexts, I've come to the conclusion that this is a wonderful pre-cursor to normal Sprint Planning. One side-effect is that it puts the initiative clearly on the team's shoulders to prepare for the Sprint while giving them scheduled time to focus and work on it. If you've been lax in grooming the Backlog in any way, this almost becomes a mandatory planning extension for your team.

Leveraging a Sprint #0

In his book on *Agile Project Management*[23], Jim Highsmith introduced the concept of running an Iteration #0. I've heard it referenced within Scrum as Sprint #0, but not formally in any of the Scrum books or primary references.

It's somewhat of a debated practice. Some think that for all project work, you should "dive into" your first Sprint and immediately begin delivering customer value. If that's truly possible, then I couldn't agree more. By customer value, I'm assuming we mean feature value. In that case, you must have a clear Backlog, a team formed and equipped, and a clear charter. So, why not dive in and start sprinting?

But what if things aren't so clear?

What if you have a new, never-been-together before team? Or, have moved members together into a new space and need to setup equipment? Or, they are embarking on a new project with no Backlog requirements or context? Or, you are being told to use a highly distributed team to get the work done? Or, your team doesn't have much Scrum experience among them, and you've just hired a brand new Scrum Master? Or, (the list goes on…)

I can think of many cases where beginning a Sprint without sufficient definition can lead to nothing productive or…Agile. It's just beginning without vision and will clearly lead to heavy requirement churn and high levels of rework.

In these cases, wouldn't it be useful to take a Sprint (or even two) to *figure things out*? At least, to get enough definition and clarity so you can begin to Sprint effectively? That's exactly the point behind a Sprint #0.

You'll want it to behave with as closely to the same dynamics as a normal, development-driven Sprint; the primary compromise usually being on delivering working software in the end. You might even want to keep the Sprint shorter to keep it more focused, and not run the risk of turning into a crutch, for Waterfall Analysis Paralysis.

---

[23] Agile Project Management is a wonderful book by Jim Highsmith that speaks to the general practices surrounding Agile PM without strong ties to any specific Agile Methodology. I've found his guidance surrounding Chartering, Agile Iterative Planning, and Iteration Types to be quite useful.

Typical activities that I've seen within a Sprint #0 include:

- Defining your High Level architecture or connections to a pre-existing Enterprise level (or other) architectures.
- Do a bit of prototyping (perhaps paper at first).
- Running User Story Writing Workshop(s) and other meetings / activities to establish your initial Product Backlog.
- Running a Backlog Grooming meeting to provide initial PBI estimates and perform release planning.
- Forming your team—introductions, establishing roles, assessing skills, etc.
- Establishing a working environment for your team—Scrum room, cubes, workstations, development and test tool servers, connections to existing tools, etc.
- Running various training sessions for your team; both technical, Scrum, and team related.
- Establishing your (Agile) project charter; then connecting it with your stakeholders.
- Perhaps conducting a project kick-off of sorts.
- Planning for, then kicking off your first Sprint…#1

One of the dangers associated with the Sprint #0, and I've already alluded to it, is that teams who are uncomfortable with ambiguity, can begin using it as an excuse for analysis paralysis. They may even want the *false comfort of too much early definition*. Therefore, you'll want to be careful that you schedule them when they are truly needed, and only continue them as long as that strong need exists.

For example, I've never seen a project that needed more than 2 – 2-week Sprint #0's to get their feet underneath them before actively Sprinting.

Exploratory 360°

Alistair Cockburn's Crystal Methodology [24] has an interesting technique that links to a Sprint #0 which I'll simply mention here. The notion is to plan an execution step to, more or less, establish your *capability* to do what you're planning to do—before you begin doing it in earnest. In other words, can you "walk your talk"?

For example, we often make assumptions that we have all the technical skills to perform our projects. What if we were planning on developing a website, but had no performance testing experience on our team? Moreover, the project was tight for time, had some relatively aggressive requirements for performance, and the testers assigned to the team kept saying—"Don't worry about it." As you can see, it's clearly a risky skill gap. But how do you handle it?

If you ran an Exploratory 360° as part of your preparation, then you'd be asking the testing team to perform some rudimentary performance testing on an existing application to get a feel for their capabilities. Clearly, surfacing whether they have the tools and expertise to do what you need them to do later on in the project.

This is the essence of it…from a risk surfacing perspective, ask your team to try some of the *hard bits* early so you can detect where the skill and capability gaps might be. After that, you'll be in a much better position to know where your teams' skills realistically stand and, if necessary, be able to plan mitigation actions.

---

[24] Crystal hasn't evolved to be a mainstream Agile Methodology. However, I find many of the techniques to be useful outside of its context and within the other methodologies. This is one of them. I've also heard this technique referred to as a Hudson's Bay Start, referenced here - http://www.striderandcline.com/hudsons.shtml so it's not solely an agile technique.

Remember

❖ Pre-vetting each Backlog Story (or item) at least 3 times will help to ensure your team is properly prepared for Sprint Planning and execution. First—when it's initially created; Second—when it's within 2-3 Sprints of execution; and Finally—when it's about to be executed within the next Sprint. Each successive drill-down provides additional clarity (descriptiveness, acceptance tests, team understanding) and better decomposition of the Story.

❖ Try to help the team focus on the Sprint Goal first, then on Stories, then on Tasks. They'll try to go too far into the details for comfort, but keep them focused on the Goal and then collaboration for the details. There's a false desire in software development for 100% clarity, which is never achieved before we begin doing the actual work. Ambiguity is something we need to become comfortable with and deal with iteratively.

❖ Never push your team too hard to cut their estimates. Teams can be quite sensitive to Product Owner pressure, both direct and more subtle and, therefore, cut estimates in order to *"appease the business"*. This will ALWAYS come back to haunt you. Instead, engage in understanding by asking good questions and careful listening. Always remind the team of the quality levels required—in order to be clear about NOT trading off Quality over Time!

Chapter 11

Sprint Execution

As a Product Owner, it's quite easy to disengage during Sprint execution because it seems as if your role gets somewhat diminished. You feel like the team is rolling along with work and you are only there to help when asked a question.

From my point of view, this is another area that can be a differentiator for a Great Product Owner. That being said, what does a Great Product Owner do during the Sprint?

Sprint Engagement

First of all, you need to fully engage with the team. Attend _all_ daily stand-ups and listen intently to what's going on. Look for opportunities to collaborate with the team each and every day. Are there testers you can sit down with to define and/or refine acceptance tests? Are there any User Stories or features approaching a demonstration state? If so, sit down with those team members and give them some early feedback. How about bugs surfacing that may need your judgment and attention? The list of activities goes on…

Remember, too, that you're a team member, so speak to your own efforts in the daily stand-up. Share your tasks, efforts, plans for that day, conversations you've had with stakeholders, etc.

Sitting with Your Team

I prefer it when Product Owners are co-located with their teams. There is no replacement for listening in on the activity – conversations, pairing, design debates, questions, comments, bugs, problems or impediments, and just being there engaging naturally and immediately, when and where you're needed within the team.

However, in some cases this is just not possible. So, the onus is on you to look for alternative strategies to support your team. Some examples include:

- If you're out of the office, dial-into all stand-ups or relevant meetings even while you're traveling.
- Establish a notion of *office hours*, where you're available for the team; I've seen an hour or two in the morning and afternoon as quite effective approaches.
- You can delegate your responsibilities, as a whole or subset, but ensure your team knows you're doing it—the details, for how long, etc. and who is representing you and in what capacity
- Even if you're remote or out of the office, regularly reach out to your team and ask if you can help; let everyone know you're available, engaged, and that you care!

I guess the point here is that _being present_, even when you're not physically there, is incredibly important to you, your team and ultimate outcomes. Stay committed to engagement and your team will sense it and respond in-kind.

Testing

In many teams the Product Owner is in a wonderful position of understanding customer needs and expectations, both at a Story level and, at a Theme level. Given that, and their need to understand Sprint progress, I usually find Great Product Owners spending considerable time testing the application.

Usually, they're working with the test team and on test-focused environments so that the software is, more often than not, a bit more mature. At regular intervals, they're checking on feature interaction and workflow—considering overall customer experience and usability of features being delivered within the Sprint.

Time and again they'll have questions and, as a result, the testing will drive healthy collaboration from the Product Owner towards the team. They're also heavily collaborating with testers on the individual Story acceptance test requirements and, if using *FitNesse*[25] or a similar tool, they're crafting their own acceptance tests for automated execution.

The key point is that testing is a natural extension of the Product Owner role and a great way to contribute to your team's efforts in a visible and high impact way. I'd really encourage this to be a part of your focus within each Sprint.

Impediments

As impediments emerge that relate to you, don't wait for the Scrum Master to track you down for follow-up action. Instead be pro-active in moving all of your personal impediment actions forward. Show the team you care by the sheer level of your attention and impediment resolution focus.

Also, stay aware of Sprint progress via your Sprint burndown charts and other team *information radiators*[26]. Stay curious; ask questions of the team about work progress and challenge them if you feel work is falling behind. If they're ahead of the Sprint Plan, certainly get ready with additional work.

If you find that a Sprint is in jeopardy and the team is falling behind, get engaged with your Scrum Master and team to figure out how you can adjust Sprint content and still meet the Sprint Goal. Be willing to listen to _all_ alternatives for changing Sprint scope, but still achieve your goals. Stay open minded. In fact, proactively suggest adjustments yourself.

---

[25] FitNesse is a tool that facilitates creating Story Acceptance Tests in HTML tables that can drive various levels of testing in your applications. It drives testing from all 'sides' of your application and is not simply UI based. The resulting test can run automatically and can become part of your regression suites. The most valuable part of FitNesse is the collaboration / communication it drives—so it creates opportunities to amplify this agile behavior. Developers, Testers, and Product Owners need to talk to get the test working!

[26] I believe Alistair Cockburn coined the term (Information Radiator) in his Crystal and Agile approaches books. An information radiator is literally any progress or state graphic that is placed in a team room for the team to view and react to. Consider them as a car dashboard, with the emphasis on reaction and adjustments.

Bugs

During the course of all software development, bugs arise. It's simply natural. In the case of Scrum and other Agile Methodologies, you want to try and resolve and/or fix all bugs as soon as they're discovered. Your team will need your help in deciding what are valid and immediate bugs versus what can be deferred. While maintaining a mindset of _Lean – Fix it Now_, help lead your team forward in balanced decision-making.

You should also be asking questions and reaffirming the quality levels of their work. I've seen many Product Owners that focus on delivering features, over delivering _High Quality_ features. You want to be a champion of the latter, and motivate the team towards this by asking quality-oriented questions. For example—"How could this set of bugs been avoided?" or, "What can we do to improve overall product quality?" This sets the tone that you're equally committed to quality as you are to production, which is an extremely important message for your team to continuously hear!

An Engagement Story

If you remember, I told a story in Chapter 9 about a start-up team that used their first Scrum sprint to target a venture capital funding event. As it turns out, their first Sprint also had a nice example of Product Owner engagement.

As you may recall, this was their very first Sprint. I had come in to give them a few hours of training, helped them craft an initial Product Backlog, facilitated Sprint Planning and assisted them with the kick-off of their first Sprint - in a matter of only a few days. Obviously, even though they were really inexperienced, they were also extremely motivated and focused on their goal.

About one week into their 4-week Sprint, while I was traveling, I received a call from their Product Owner, at 5 a.m. (west coast time) regarding their burndown chart. It seemed that they were not burning down as expected and it appeared as if they weren't going to make their goal. However, when challenged on their progress, the team spoke of dependencies and how things were actually nicely on-track. I suggested that he continue to probe his team, and wait a few days—trusting their guidance.

When they did get the burndown to represent their real progress a few days later, things were much better aligned. However, it did appear like they *would only get about 80% of their User Stories complete. This was a real problem given the fact that additional VC funding was riding on their Story content.*

On the very next day, the Product Owner gave me a call (again, 5 a.m. on west coast time), but hey... he had a Sprint progress observation and wanted my advice. He said it seemed clear that the team was going to miss delivering some of the features for the Sprint. However, he was OK with that and wanted to know if he could start removing or reframing Stories in order to increase the teams ability to meet the Sprint Goal? So, here's a Product Owner who, in their very first Sprint, <u>gets</u> the difference between <u>planned scope</u> versus <u>actual team capacity</u> and the need for ongoing adjustments. Ah Ha—I thought!

Also, based on internal demonstrations, he wanted to know if he could change some Story characteristics to make their overall demo more powerful—thus, supporting the Sprint Goal. I said sure! Work with your team and figure out the requisite changes to have an outrageously successful funding demo. The sooner, the better!

It seemed the Product Owner "got" the whole Scrum customer engagement model and dynamically worked with his team to adjust—based on progress discovery and feedback on how to creatively and realistically create a compelling demo. To complete the story—the team successfully garnered their funding. Even more compelling to me was how immediately and well the Product Owner engaged Agility and his team. Now, that's a Product Owner on the verge of Greatness!

Adjusting the Sprint?

Quite often Sprints don't turn out as planned and something needs to be adjusted in the middle of things. One reason might be to make priority changes, based on external customer changes, to the contents of the Sprint. Another is when the team finds itself struggling with their original commitment to the work—if they either under or overestimated things. And another reason is that software is by definition a challenging endeavor and, therefore, sometimes unexpected risks may surface. We're going to explore a few scenarios here.

One important point is that none of these actions are solely the responsibility of the Product Owner. In fact, the leader here should be the Scrum Master. He or she is your partner and should guide you in making any necessary adjustments, etc. However, you do play a significant part in the Sprint _recovery_ process, too!

Content Disconnect

The team is struggling to deliver the Sprint contents. Within the first few days of the Sprint, you and the Scrum Master realize that an adjustment is necessary. I've seen several approaches to this. Classically, Scrum allows for cancelling and re-planning your Sprint. That works well if you're a stand-alone team. However, if your team is synchronized with others, then this approach can be awkward in that you'll need to plan a reduced length Sprint in order to maintain your synchronization.

Another approach is to simply run a re-planning meeting. This is where the team, given the recent discoveries, tries to maximize delivery of content towards the original Sprint Goal. Since you're using the previous Sprint Backlog as a baseline, this is usually a quick meeting where you and the team figure out the best game plan for the Sprint. If done soon enough, within the first 1-3 days of a two week Sprint, I've seen teams significantly recover their progress and often meet the original Sprint goal.

Priority Disconnect

One of my favorite Product Owners struggled with changing his mind quite often within Sprints. We were working on an eCommerce SaaS application where "things changed" often due to customer and market dynamics. In these cases, he was more likely to cancel the Sprint and then re-plan a new one based on a major priority shift in the Backlog. However, when re-planning we tried to stay open minded about integrating the new work and maintaining some of the original Sprint focus.

Another aspect of this is insufficient look-ahead. I was never convinced that we couldn't anticipate these changes in some way. Remember, we were on a 2 week Sprint model which is fairly nimble. As we'll discuss next, looking ahead and anticipating events is another important activity during Sprint execution.

Looking Ahead

Another place to invest time with your team and each Sprint is *"looking ahead"* in anticipation of future actions. For example:

- ✓ Ensure the team reserves time during each Sprint for Backlog grooming activity. Then, actively schedule Backlog grooming and estimation meetings as required.
- ✓ Examine the team's velocity within the Sprint, also considering past Sprint velocity. If they're going to have problems delivering in this Sprint, get engaged in making appropriate adjustments.
- ✓ Adjust the Backlog based on velocity vs. delivered value vs. release plans vs. your budget. Always remember, it's a dynamic list!
- ✓ Remind team members to add, change, break down, combine, and remove items from the Backlog; to proactively manage it with you.
- ✓ Potentially remove items from the Backlog that may be too large, too future oriented, lack relevancy or, in general, dilute the team's attention.
- ✓ Getting the Backlog Stories ready for the next Sprint and developing a new Sprint Goal.
- ✓ If you're working in an environment with multiple Scrum teams and cross-Backlog dependencies, ensure your collaboration across the PO organization.

These are all activities that you should be engaging in with your team.

Preparing for the Sprint Review

During the Sprint, you should also be monitoring progress on a Story-by-Story basis and mapping progress to the overall burndown to get a feel whether the Sprint will be successful or not; in other words, preparing for the Sprint Review. One of the core tenants of agility is delivering and demonstrating *working software* which should happen in Scrum in the Sprint review; this is where we're going next…

Remember

❖ Stay fully engaged in the Sprints and attend all daily Scrum meetings. Listen to the "progress pulse" from the team, and always be ready to make adjustments, while looking for opportunities where you might be able to help.

❖ Sitting with your team during the Sprint can make a huge difference. Even if it's part-time and scheduled, it will show you're engaged and foster collaboration with your team.

❖ Get involved with all aspects of "Testing the App" within the Sprint. You're not only testing; you're engaging and providing wonderful feedback!

❖ "Look ahead" as much as possible within the Sprint towards future Sprints. Engage the team in Backlog grooming and estimation meetings and/or activities; this will help avoid the Sprint-by-Sprint vision that undermines many team's potential.

Chapter 12

The Sprint Review—A Defining Moment!

Transparency is certainly one of the keys to effective performance of your agile teams. One of the best Scrum mechanisms for exposing your team's results is the Sprint Review. It supports some of the basic tenants of agility by:

Demonstrating working software (potentially shippable product increment) to your Customer and gaining their Acceptance of your work.

The Sprint Review really is a defining moment for the team and the place where value is demonstrated. It shouldn't be construed as a "Dog and Pony Show", or contrived demonstration of software that may crash at any moment. Instead, the software features should be robust and well behaved.

It's not necessarily highly polished. I've seen FitNesse test (fixtures, test cases, execution) demonstrations that weren't very powerful or slick. However, they contained tremendous value from a business and quality perspective and we endeavored to get that point across. Incidentally, we executed the tests.

Even though the Sprint Review is a holistic team event, I would like to now share a few focus points that Great Product Owners can, and should, bring to the table for a powerful and defining moment to conclude each and every Sprint.

Taking Ownership for Attendance

It's crucial that you get the right business stakeholders and other interested parties in the Sprint Review. It's important from a team morale perspective, from a transparency perspective, and it's also important from a feedback perspective.

I've seen patterns where attendance is spotty in reviews. Sometimes there is good engagement and, at other times, there's not. Every so often, we would send out the meeting invitations late, even though it's a regularly scheduled event tempo and this would drastically affect attendance. Or, we wouldn't effectively explain what was on the agenda for the review.

Where sometimes colleagues who are customer-facing and who would find great value in the review, aren't included or don't attend. Often times, if key participants can't attend, they neglect to send an advocate or a delegate.

All of these symptoms indicate a lack of preparation and engagement on the part of the Product Owner. The Sprint Review is the _defining moment_ for the team's work, including your own, at the end of each Sprint. It is absolutely unacceptable to do a shoddy job of getting the right people there—on time and excited about the possibilities.

I have no _special tricks_ [27] to provide, nor silver bullets, simply the council to take ownership of attendance. Please take it seriously. Personally invite participants, preferably face-to-face and then by follow-up email. Follow-up if they don't attend. I'd even go so far as to say it's an _impediment_ if attendance is poor on a regular basis and would consider it an indicator that the project lacks value and/or importance.

---

[27] While it's not a special trick, I'd suggest you ask key stakeholders and customers why they're not attending and work with you Scrum Master and team to adjust as much as possible to their feedback. Another idea is to schedule Sprint Reviews only when there's something significant to demonstrate. I see this problem in teams with shorter Sprint cycles, say 1-2 weeks. It's sometimes difficult to have 'enough' functionality after such a short period. In these cases, I recommend common sense and scheduling reviews when you do have more meaningful content. Perhaps scheduling a more internally focused review for the team when you don't.

Helping the Team to Prepare

The Agile and Scrum methods demand working, demonstrable software whenever possible. Be firm in this respect! Sit down with anyone who is orchestrating the meeting and discuss how you can make a good impression—effectively illustrating the work and the business value that the team has provided.

Not every Sprint Review needs to follow the same *script*. In fact, you may want to vary things to keep your audiences coming back for more. In many ways this is a marketing effort for you and your team, so activate your marketing skills, albeit for internal use.

I've seen the following general game plan used *successfully* in many teams and it may serve to drive your thinking as well. Oh, and one more thing, you're simply helping the team prepare a *High Impact* review here. The overall review is the team's responsibility to prepare, including the Product Owner and Scrum Master, so it should be very much a collaborative effort.

1. **Discussion:** About half way through the Sprint, you might start discussing the review amongst the team in your stand-ups and other venues. This not only gets everyone thinking of the Sprint Review planning, but it also focuses them on driving Sprint results.

2. **Create a Script:** I usually ask the team to start thinking about the Sprint Review 'script' that we'll be following in the review. Having a plan for this is imperative. How will you kick-off the review and who will do it? What will the Story / Feature flow look like? What's the timing—so that everything 'fits' in your time-box? Who will facilitate? I've found that members of the test team enjoy pulling this together and they usually have a more holistic view to the story the Sprint Goal is trying to tell.

3. **Practice:** Again, you might not always need this and I'm certainly not recommending 8 hours of practice for a 1 hour Sprint Review. However, you don't want to come unprepared and/or send *that* message to your stakeholder colleagues either. So, depending on the content, you might want to gather the team and practice your 'script'.

4. **Delivery:** If you've done 1...3, then this is easy. Otherwise...good luck!

Targeting the Impact – It's Not Only the Features…

I sometimes like to dig a little deeper and demonstrate other things in the review besides just features or Stories. I brought up an example of this in the introduction of the chapter that related to FitNesse tests. Not only do you want to demonstrate the functionality, but in cases where the value proposition isn't quite clear to the layman stakeholder, you or another member of the team should explain the value or the point in terms that are the most meaningful.

Continued Story

Continuing from that FitNesse point in the chapter introduction…

One team I was coaching was working on a suite of eCommerce applications. There were parts of the internal logic for one application component that was simply too difficult to test thoroughly. This lack of quality had been frustrating us literally for years! It also surfaced some damaging defects in our customer releases. However, in our case, these bugs could result in lost revenue and/or increased costs to our customers that we'd have to compensate them for—so a very real business impact!

The problem was time and complexity. In order to test all of the permutations of logic, we calculated it would take several hundred thousand test cases that might (a pure guess here folks) take weeks, or even months, to execute; we clearly never had the time for it. What could we do?

First, one of our testers used a testing tool call AllPairs to winnow down the important test cases to a "manageable" set of several hundred tests.

Then, the team went about automating all of those via FitNesse tests in a single Sprint. Along the way, they came across three critical bugs that our customers hadn't found yet and immediately fixed them. At the end of the Sprint, we had a fully operational set of automated FitNesse tests that thoroughly tested one of our most complex sub-systems. Thus, freeing us to work on more important future Stories AND, assuring our customers (and our bank account) wouldn't be affected by this component again.

When we evaluated this in the Sprint Review, we needed to" set the stage" for the audience, to clarify exactly what we had done. We also needed to explain its significance from a business perspective. Once we did that, everyone applauded the effort. I could even see a serious sparkle in the eye of our CEO.

Meeting Dynamics

Here are just a few points that I've found to drive successful Sprint Review results and impressions…

Setting the Stage

I believe it's the Product Owner's responsibility to set the stage in the Sprint Review. He/she should get up and explain what their goal(s) are for the Sprint. He or she should also to be able to share and express their views as to how the team responded to the challenge.

If the team struggled in the beginning of the Sprint with getting focused, but mid-way came together and ultimately delivered towards the Goal and 85% of the planned content, then say that. If they exceeded the Sprint plan by another 5 User Stories, exhausting your stretch items, then say that as well. Paint a brief, but accurate, assessment of the *team's journey through the Sprint* for the audience.

It's also important to reiterate your thinking behind the Sprint Goal. What business strategy did you have in mind? What are the critical business and customer drivers? Strongly frame the work that everyone is about to see within a business context.

Not a Demo, Not a Show and Tell; Instead—Valuable and Working Software

This is my experience and background showing through, so bear with me. I've been part of many a contrived system demo or a software show-and-tell. While these were well intentioned events, they often demonstrated software of low quality. For example, our demo scripts were littered with functions and operations to avoid or, we had setup the database and data to be simple and correct—just for the demo.

Don't fall into that trap in your review. While you may be delivering Stories with limited scope, you should never alter their quality; they should work under all functional conditions. Ensure that your Sprint Review conditions (systems, people, and execution) amplify quality and, subsequently, _your confidence_.

In addition, take the time to demonstrate your User Story acceptance criteria with each feature or story. Better that you've automated them, so a simple quick run of the tests with, hopefully, _Green_ indications that have all passed. If they haven't already been automated, at least run through them as part of the exposure of each story. I always like the notion of closing the demonstration of each feature with either a firm acceptance (Yes) or give reasons why it deviates from your expectations (No or Maybe).

And between us, the latter should never occur as a surprise within the demo itself!

The Whole Team

The best Sprint Reviews I've attended are those where the entire team participated in the review—everyone showing their work. It may create a bit of a hand-off challenge as laptops are exchanged and people move into the _hot seat_, but the effect is powerful in that the entire team is involved (as Pigs) in what's going on.

If someone is anxious and neglects pointing out, or demonstrating an important detail, another person on the team comfortably jumps in and covers it for them. Why? Because they're a team and everyone is aware of the overall deliverables. Everyone clearly understands each Stories relationship towards the business value and Sprint Goals.

I strongly recommend a holistic team approach to your reviews, but do it within the context of your team's comfort and ability.

Calling it!

This is an area where I may split with conventional wisdom in the Scrum community. I like having the Product Owner declare victory (or defeat) as an outcome of the Sprint Review. That is, if the team delivered on the Goal, then say the Sprint was a _Success_. If they did not deliver sufficient quality or content to meet the Goal, then say the Sprint _Failed_. While this may be a gray area decision and not a binary or arbitrary decision, I want the decision to be made and stated within the review.

Not berating the team, not apologizing, but in simple, transparent terms—honestly and respectfully, telling it like it is.

And again, this should never come as a surprise to the Scrum Master or your team but be more so an extension of the everyday discussions amongst the team—representing their ultimate Sprint deliverables.

And Afterwards…Reflection

Lest I forget, there are really two crucial ceremonies at the end of each Sprint. So far we've discussed the Sprint Review. However, there's an equally important event that requires the Product Owners attention as well—the Sprint Retrospective.

The retrospective setup and facilitation is in the realm of the Scrum Master. However, as the Product Owner and team member, you owe it to yourself to fully participate in the retrospective. While this is always vital, it's particularly important if the Sprint didn't go well or failed to meet your expectations.

The retrospective is the one venue for you to raise points and issues of concern, both good and bad, from your particular functional perspective. Usually, the retrospective is a private event—including only the team. For that reason, it's a good place for private and challenging conversations as a team member. To be honest, I see too many Product Owners missing this opportunity to give feedback to their teams. They simply _go along for the ride_ and avoid the difficult or meaningful conversations, seeming to prefer being perceived as a _nice guy or gal_. Nothing could be more wasteful.

As I've said before in this guide, agile transparency is in all directions. Your role as a Great Product Owner requires you to express to your team the reality of their performance as it relates to external expectations and business needs. It's also to effectively evaluate their results in delivering value to you as a representative of the business. Please don't miss your opportunity to provide congruent team feedback via the Sprint Retrospective.

Remember

❖ By mid-Sprint begin assessing your delivery and planning for the Sprint Review. I've found testers sometimes enjoy the "Master of Ceremony" role in the review, i.e., _conducting_ it.

❖ Leverage a team-based approach for delivering features within the Review and have individuals demonstrate their _wares_. This level of accountability and transparency will increase overall Done-Ness and quality.

❖ Always ensure you've explained in layman's terms the business value you've delivered to your Sprint Review audience. Not only in the invitation agenda, but again in the Review itself. In many ways, you're "selling" it to them—so don't be afraid to sell!

❖ Don't be afraid to call your Sprint a Success or Failure. Explain why in either case; then inspect, move forward and adapt, as necessary. In fact, you should clearly understand this _before_ the Review—so plan your assessment and reactions with your Chief Product Owner and Scrum Master.

Chapter 13

The Product Owner as Leader

One of the more misunderstood parts of the Product Owner role is that of team leadership. Whenever I instantiate Scrum within an organization, I try to establish the Scrum Master and the Product Owner as leadership roles within their teams. I know, I know, agile teams are self-directed, but I've found it helps for both of these roles to understand the fundamentals of *Servant Leadership* [28] and to truly engage in leading their teams— particularly, early on within their agile adoption.

I believe that a Great Product Owner must have innate leadership abilities or, at least, be willing to work on improving them as they develop and grow within their roles. Beyond themselves, they need to establish a leadership *partnership* of sorts with their Scrum Masters.

Understanding <u>your</u> Team

I've worked with some Product Owners who don't become intimate with their teams capabilities and capacity. In other words, they don't get to *know* their team. Instead, they often allow the insatiable demands of the business, for more features than the team is capable of, to transparently pass through them and become frustrated and/or overly demanding with their teams.

---

[28] Robert K. Greenleaf initiated the Servant Leadership movement in 1964 inspired by his work at AT&T. He wrote widely on the subject and, to my way of thinking, is still the leading author on the subject. You hear his philosophy quoted widely in the agile management & leadership community.

Keep in mind there's a huge difference in driving the team with *BHAG*[29] goals and constantly, stubbornly demanding extra effort and work than is clearly feasible. The former is related to becoming more intimate with your teams capacity, but slightly pushing them to do more than they think is possible. While the latter is Waterfall and traditional leadership at it's worst.

Every Product Owner has a responsibility to become intimate with the capacity of their teams along the lines of understanding:

- What is their overall velocity Sprint-over-Sprint?
- Who are the strongest team members?
- Who are the technical and thought leaders?
- Who are the weakest team members? In what areas (technically and softer skills)?
- From a complimentary skills perspective, where are the strengths and gaps?
- What do they 'like' to do vs. not like to do?
- What motivates the individuals? And the team as a whole?

You also have a responsibility to understand the same factors for yourself and your Scrum Master. Then, after having all of this team and self-realization information, factor this into your *thinking* around Product Backlog organization, Sprint Planning, Goal Setting, and external collaboration with stakeholders to discuss the team's capabilities and capacities.

One compelling reason for all of this reflection is to foster the passion and creative energy of your team. Agile teams don't necessarily go faster than their traditional counterparts. Instead, one of the speed attributes of agility is creatively and energetically solving problems—with solutions that are simple and creative, while truly addressing the challenges you've presented to the team. Only by getting to know your team, can you frame your Backlog and challenges to foster an environment where this culture *emerges* from within the team.

---

[29] Big Hairy Audacious Goal; a "stretch" goal of sorts. I don't believe Great Product Owners should be motivating their team with soft or easily achieved goals. They should inspire the team and having them require some extra effort is part of that inspiration.

Fostering Transparency

One of the ongoing insights I have within my agile team leadership journey is continually realizing the awesome power of transparency. It's something that cuts through all of the traditional Waterfall *management speak*, for example—"Lets get this project back on schedule".

Excuse me, but it was never ON schedule! Instead, it's exactly where it was supposed to be given the challenges and our investment. The key isn't holding to some arbitrary schedule, the key is adjusting to discoveries as you focus in on your goal or target, and delivering the highest value features without quality compromises.

Part of being transparent is sharing your team's activity, and discussing this activity with your stakeholders as a natural course of project events. Not via specialized status reports, but by communicating with them on a day-to-day basis:

- Asking them to walk-around the team's work area—to review Backlogs, Plans, Burn-downs, etc.
- Inviting them to attend daily stand-ups and to genuinely listen to the team's efforts and progress.
- Inviting them to Sprint Planning or Backlog grooming and estimation meetings.
- Also, ensuring that they are included in (and attend) every Sprint Review.

I've found that over time stakeholders can mistake the value and opportunity of Sprint Reviews and, therefore, their attendance can be spotty or wane. Nothing can be more dangerous to your team's transparency. Project state information in agile teams is most effectively shared via face-to-face interactions. As part of your role and planning for a Sprint Review, ensure that you've invited, and have reinforced the value, of stakeholder attendance. If they need to be there…get them there!

Share good news with them wherever and whenever possible. I've found many of us like to give a lot of attention to the bad news. Try not to solely focus on those issues. Share with them about how hard the team is working to solve problems and overcoming obstacles, as well as, how creative and energetic they are in attacking risks. Also, share with them about how much they're getting done and/or how much more is getting done then they originally planned or anticipated.

Of course you'll want to disclose the challenges facing the team, but always in the light of early discovery and adjustment. Remember, by the time bad news is revealed in traditional teams, it's often too late to take corrective action and still hold onto your targets. In Scrum teams you'll be getting _discovery on a daily basis_. Get ready for it. You'll know what's right and what's wrong in weeks or even months before you'd have discovered it in a traditional project.

You'll also be closer to the root cause of each challenge—so your corrective actions are more discrete and targeted towards solutions. Help your team and, more importantly, your stakeholders to realize that this level of transparency, while perhaps frightening and overwhelming at times, is _much different and much better_ than their traditional experiences.

Finally, remember that your Scrum Master is your partner in this transparency endeavor, so please don't go it alone. You both should be planning to ensure that _all_ aspects of your team's and projects' progress is boldly available in real-time for analysis by everyone. Be an open book in everything you do and always be honest.

Championing your Team

A huge part of becoming a Great Product Owner is aligning with, and becoming an advocate for, your team. This doesn't come for free. Nor, does it happen immediately. It will take effort on your part to learn, understand, and grow to trust one another.

As I said earlier, the first step is to become familiar with your team—their strengths, weaknesses, personality types, etc. You'll want to spend some time during work, as well as, off-hour times socializing with, and getting to know, each of them. _Breaking bread_ [30] is a wonderful way to establish a strong team bond. This is a critical step that will pay ongoing dividends from a teamwork and business value delivery perspective.

---

[30] Joel on Software speaks to having lunch each day with his teams as an approach to build teamwork and cross-team collaboration. I've seen this referenced elsewhere and seen it work personally.

At every opportunity, you need to become a _Voice_ for your team. When they're winning—shout it out! When they need help with a project, work with the Scrum Master to go out and get it. When they've "_Leaped Tall Buildings in a Single Bound_", make sure everyone knows that relative to their capacity or capability, this team is "Rockin"!

Most importantly, if your team needs you, always support them. No matter what else is on your plate, you need to be there for them—delivering on all aspects of your role. This may mean you have to either delegate tasks to other team members to help out, or to say "no" to your manager concerning other Product Management tasks. Have the _courage_[31] to do what is best for your team!

Setting a Leadership Example

There are four areas that come to mind when I think of Great Product Owners setting a solid leadership example within their teams…

Taking on Work

I love it when the Product Owner takes on tasks within a Sprint. We handle these as we would with any team member—with visibility and movement towards getting the work done. Often, the work has dependencies to other team members, so this puts delivery pressure on the Product Owner.

While the role is truly different, being a good team player and member is about helping each other out. It's useful to actually look for opportunities whenever you can; I normally see them exist in these following areas:

- Doing extra work to refine and add color to Backlog items.
- Working with team members on individual User Stories; perhaps even signing up for specific tasks.
- Always being available to review Stories and Acceptance Tests as they develop—providing ongoing feedback.

---

[31] If you skipped over the Introduction and first two chapters, you might want to go back their and read about the breadth of the Product Manager/Owner roles. If you're a Product Manager, there's typically an awful lot on your plate—so this can be a particularly hard stance for you…

- Trying to have time where you sit with your team; better that it be full-time, but regular *office hours* work well too.
- Writing acceptance tests and performing informal functional testing.

Keep it in the Family

Perhaps it's just the teams I've been associated with over the past few years, but I've seen a pattern emerge from certain Product Owners. They speak poorly about their teams to executives and other stakeholders. They generally fall into this pattern when the team hasn't delivered what is expected of them. Normally, these expectations are not driven by transparent team capacity, but instead by traditional management, demand-based thinking, pushing the team towards a perceived capacity that is unrealistic and unhealthy.

Another aspect of this pattern is that Product Owners don't share their pressure and insight with their teams. Instead, they silently operate as if everything is going well and communicate to their teams that they're quite satisfied with the ongoing progress. I'm guessing this has something to do with conflict avoidance or, perhaps, background and/or culture.

I can't tell you how disruptive this is. First, they're not being good teammates or operating effectively within their role. Secondly, they're not defending their team and speaking to the real challenges that are being faced. Finally, they are simply not being trustworthy. Trust me—the team will be aware of it. Watch out for this pattern and always try to deal with your teams and your projects congruently—openly and in a trustworthy manor.

Challenge your Teams!

In regards to the former section, Great Product Owners challenge their teams. The first place to do this is with Sprint Goals. I literally hate it when a Product Owner comes into a Sprint Planning meeting with a flat, simple, non-compelling goal. It means they have no excitement, drive or vision, for the Sprint—yet they expect the team to energetically respond.

Instead, try to bring in something that will get the team motivated and get their blood pumping. It should be *demanding* and should challenge the team's capabilities at every turn. The term "Stretch Goal" comes to mind often—in that it should S-T-R-E-T-C-H the team—enabling them to grow and excel. Another way to think about it is that every Sprint should feel somewhat uncomfortable to them. It should create tension, as well as, excitement! They should perhaps feel just a little nervous -- like somehow they may not succeed. These are, what I believe to be, the dynamics of solid Sprint Goals.

I've seen a pattern in Sprint Planning where the team will plan a Sprint only up to their capacity. Everyone will take on 100% of what they think they can deliver and then stop. This isn't a bad practice at all—particularly when you consider most engineers' propensity to underestimate their work.

However, a better practice is to identify stretch stories for the Sprint, task them out, and place the Stories/tasks on the Sprint Board for the Sprint. The team buys into them as _Stretch Items_ for this Sprint while everyone tries to accomplish the planned work, as well as the stretch items. In my experience, mature Scrum teams will get to and complete the stretch items…and beyond -- 80% of the time.

A Not so "Challenging" Story

On one occasion, I attended a presentation that a Product Owner was making to a group of sales people. It was a quarterly presentation where he was relating development progress against his last few quarterly promises. In many cases, he was falling back on those promises and, as you can imagine, the sales force was annoyed and gave him a great deal of grief. They were frustrated because they had to again go out and explain to customers that many of the features that were sorely needed in their product were delayed. The Product Owner tried to explain the difficulties to everyone, but in the end, everyone was discouraged with the lack of perceived progress.

Please understand, the agile teams were executing well…very well in this case and delivering release-over-release value. It was just that external expectations were not being met. (Are they ever?) Unfortunately, they were not being set very effectively in this case either.

I followed him back into his Scrum team over the next week or so and noticed that not one word of those challenging and frustrating conversations was being shared with them. This was such a waste! He was a part of this team and transparency needed to go both ways. The team needed to hear that there were problems and frustrations and to realize they were not meeting external expectations. They also needed to consider what parts they could play to respond to those expectations—as a team.

In this case, I felt the Product Owner should have been much more transparent in sharing the good news as well as the bad. He should have also expressed the personal frustration he felt in translating the team's work towards meeting sales expectations. To my thinking this was a wasted opportunity in engaging his team.

Your <u>Partner</u>

Great Product Owners establish a partnership with their Scrum Masters. The two of you are really the central leadership influences within your team. Clearly, your role is *more externally focused*, while the role of the Scrum Master is *more team or internally focused*.

You should observe this partnership to distinguish how you both can serve and coach your team to even greater performance. Also, explore how you can remove impediments that are blocking their efforts—jointly focusing your teams on producing technically excellent results, delivering ultra high quality software, and working towards gaining highly effective teamwork and collaboration.

A word on impediments -- they're not just needs from the team that are raised in the daily stand-up! The most important impediments are the more subtle ones that the Scrum Master and Product Owner observe from their team's behaviors and delivery patterns, including:

- Your team isn't collaborating effectively—for example, developers are throwing work "over the wall" to testers or the testers aren't embracing agile collaboration with you or the developers.

- You don't have sufficient time to be a Great Product Owner; the Scrum Master isn't focused full-time on their team. In general, solid agile practice coaching and preparation is being ignored.

- Nobody is addressing under-performers and performance issues—technical skill (programming skill, automation skills, domain knowledge, deliverable quality, etc.) within the team.

- Addressing under performance and performance issues—soft skills (collaboration, teamwork, transparency, and attitude) across the team.

- Stakeholders are expecting too much; asking the wrong questions, for example—"Are you on schedule for 100% of the scope?"

- Team attrition—lack of fun and fulfilling work; too much by-rote activity; addressing burnout—everyone working too hard.

- Significant quality issues – team compromising quality over scope/time; a general lack of adherence to good agile quality practices and missing or ignoring your Done-Ness and other Criteria.

All of the above are simple examples of the kinds of impediments that I'd expect (fully partnered and collaborating) Scrum Masters and Product Owners to be coaching *and leading* their teams through. I'm going to say something quite contentious here. I think the notion of s*elf-direction*, which is, of course, central to great agile teams, is something that doesn't occur by accident. I think it's something that's coached, coaxed, guided, fostered, exampled, and led by you and the Scrum Master along with your teams.

The central theme in this chapter is that I fervently believe a Great Product Owner plays a role in *leading* that evolution.

Remember

❖ Get to know the strengths and characteristics of your team; then leverage that knowledge in crafting Backlog work that maps between Business Needs, while leveraging the skills and strengths of your team.

❖ Share your thoughts and challenges with your team. Bring them up to speed on business dynamics and the competitive landscape. Also share internal pressures. Be clear and honest with them. Push them to be their best and deliver towards these pressures.

❖ Engage with your team. Pitch in and help and lead by example. Truly partner with your Scrum Master and endeavor to be a Servant Leader—doing whatever it takes to support your team.

Chapter 14

Understanding How Your Role Influences Quality

Maintaining ongoing product or application quality is one of the central themes within the agile methods. I remember the keynote presentation that Robert, 'Uncle Bob', Martin gave at the Agile 2008 Conference. It was entitled _Quintessence_. In it, he was lamenting the need for a fifth addition to the Agile Manifesto that emphasized _Craftsmanship over Crap_[32]. The essence of the presentation was the need for a relentless focus on professionalism and craftsmanship on the part of every agile team member.

The point being that quality is the responsibility of every team member. That it shouldn't enter a developer's mind to deliver a component that hasn't been properly designed or unit tested. It shouldn't enter the tester's mind to skip over testing functions that have clear value to the customers. It also shouldn't enter a Product Owner's mind to blindly demand features from their team or to challenge their estimates and integrity. Furthermore, she shouldn't ask for hacked up features—simply to meet a date.

The team is expected to maintain the integrity of their craftsmanship regardless of any force that drives them towards delivering crap. More so

---

[32] http://blog.objectmentor.com/articles/2008/08/14/quintessence-the-fifth-element-for-the-agile-manifesto . I found the entire Keynote to be a call to arms for a pattern I've seen in quite a few agile teams. Teams have been too long blaming 'them' for their own quality compromises and sprint failures. 'They' could be the Scrum Master, Product Owner, and clearly business stakeholders and executives. Bob made the point though that each individual and the team as a whole are responsible for their work and their compromises. That if lines need to be held, they should be responsible and hold to them.

than you might imagine, I believe the Great Product Owner plays a fundamental role in this endeavor; we'll explore those aspects next.

Let's Be Clear, You Don't Test In Quality

I spend a great deal of time coaching various teams in their agile adoption and make this point in every introductory class. But, inevitably after we're done sprinting, I hear team members, cross-functional stakeholders, and executives talking about testing and quality as if they were synonymous.

Read my lips. _You don't test in quality_. By the time you get to testing, it's too late. Your quality has already been instantiated into your code. Instead, build quality into your DNA and work by individually adopting some of these core values:

- Build quality into your Stories by sitting down with actual customers and precisely understanding their challenges and usage.
- Make your Product Backlogs transparent and easily available to everyone. Encourage questions and feedback.
- Listen deeply to your stakeholders and understand their priorities and needs.
- Build quality into your code by collaborating and pairing while performing more formal code reviews whenever possible— particularly, on the more complex sections or areas where you're in unfamiliar territory.
- If you encounter some horrible pre-existing code or hacks, consistently endeavor to re-factor and improve or simplify them. Always leave the code better "after you're gone".
- Take the time to create thoughtful tests at every level (unit, feature, system, regression) and then relentlessly test as early as possible.
- Automate all tests so you can run them quickly—achieving continuous feedback on your changes.
- If you do decide to 'skip' work at any level, place it on the Backlog for future clean-up and improvement. Make the trade-off transparent.
- Never blame management, or others, for the lack of quality. Instead, as part of your team, professionally hold yourself accountable to the highest principles and standards.

Aspects of Quality

So, what did the previous list imply? Hopefully, the implication was that quality does not equal testing. While testing IS an important part of the equation, it is certainly not all of it.

As you define your Product Backlog (requirements), you are building quality into the system. Every debate that you have within your team concerning requirements—how to implement them and how to make them simpler and more directed towards the customers' needs, will improve your quality.

Every session you have in which you engage with customers to truly understand their business and operational needs, will improve the quality of the requirements. You do this, not only for your customer, but to improve the quality of the requirements presented to your team.

Within software development itself, there are critical quality points. The early emphasis points include architecture, design collaboration, and inspection. At times, it appears as if the Agile Methodologies don't sufficiently stress good software design. By the time you reach the system level, component level, and individual feature level, the team should be engaged in collaborative design and team reviews. Even as they increment the design, this should be happening in thin slices of end-to-end behavior. Everyone should understand and be able to follow the overall system design, which leads to simpler designs and easier cross-team implementations.

Another critical quality step is code reviews and/or inspections. A big part of XP's Pair Programming practice is focused towards inspection-like activity, acknowledging that two sets of eyes are better than one. The other important aspect in reviews is catching errors or bugs early, when they are the easiest and cheapest to resolve.

Testing is still a quality practice, simply not the only one. Within agile teams, I've noticed a narrowing in testing focus. It's typically driven from the Unit, Story + Acceptance, and Story – Functional Behavior perspectives. This, more or less, ensures that the Backlog deliverables are working. However, there is much more to testing than simply qualifying the individual features. Later on in this chapter, I'll try to expand the definition of testing so that you consider its broadly nuanced depth and breadth when constructing your Backlog and performing release planning.

Finally, agile Continuous Integration and Automated Testing practices provide the safety-net that is needed to be able to make small, fast system changes or extensions, and get real-time feedback on results. Many think that their focus should be on speed. Actually, the automation investment in the agile methods is related to feedback, since we're trying to make those small incremental changes as quickly and as safely as possible. Driving quality before speed!

Traditional & Agile Quality Practices

The assumption is often made by many people outside the agile community that the Agile Methods are not a quality play. The reality is quite the opposite. Many of the practices do not resemble their Waterfall equivalents. *Figure 9* lists the traditional quality practices and tries to correlate them to their agile counterparts. This list isn't necessarily complete, but it does give you a sense for the type of quality practices that should be occurring within your teams.

Traditional Quality Approaches or Practices	Agile Practices with a Similar Focus
Requirement Gathering	Conducting User Story writing workshops and collaborative Product Backlog construction
Requirement Qualification	Running Sprint Reviews with customers present; adapting to feedback with reduced change cost
Code Inspection or Reviews	Pair Programming; Pair Testing; using collaborative tools for distributed reviews
Code Quality	TDD or Unit Testing practices; Pairing developers and testers
Quality Control, process-driven practices, checklists, repositories,	Applying Lean practices in software development; emphasizing Professionalism & Craftsmanship within the team

Figure 9a, Examples of Traditional Quality Practices and their Agile Counterparts

Traditional Quality Approaches or Practices	Agile Practices with a Similar Focus
Configuration Management Processes	Continuous Integration as a practice; fixing broken builds in a stop-the-line fashion; Transparency
Risk Management practices	Iteratively inspecting results; raising risks and immediately dealing with them within the team
Plan documents (Project, Test, Documentation, Development, Overall); Project Schedules	Minimal planning – overlay the Backlog via Release Planning; Face-to-face communication on steps; Scrum of Scrums for dependency coordination
Requirement Traceability	Numbering stories and acceptance tests; keeping track of pass/fail rates per User Story
Project and other status reporting	Transparency; Wiki's, Burndowns, maintaining other Information Radiators in the Team room
Defect Triage; Change Control Boards	Fixing defects individually—at the most responsible moment; deferring few bugs
Architecture and Design Reviews	Incremental or emergent practices— delivering features as end-to-end, thin slices of functionality; simply, metaphors for system architecture and flow

Figure 9b, Examples of Traditional Quality Practices and their Agile Counterparts

Next, I want to discuss the role that the Great Product Owner has in collaborating with team members—without negatively influencing their work quality.

Don't Push Compromise—Instead Trust

As a Product Owner, you have to walk a fine line between asking your teams to explain and quantify their quality decisions, yet not push them too hard and drive quality compromises into their work.

In the first edition of _Extreme Programming_ by Kent Beck, he drew a clear and stark distinction between the role of the customer (Product Owner) and the role of the team. In it, he emphasized that the customer drove work prioritization, scope trade-off decisions, and then finally, accepted the team's work.

But Beck emphasized that teams made the technical decisions surrounding architecture and design. Ultimately, while you can explore various design aspects with the team and discuss trade-offs, once it was decided _what was wanted/needed,_ they were responsible for _how it was to be implemented_. They were also responsible for _how long it would take_. He also reminded us that good agile customers always kept in mind that team estimates were even more sacrosanct than their designs.

This stark delineation came out of respect for each of our professional experience and roles. Kent alluded to the team's need to respect and value the customer role within the team. Yes, debate scope definition and data requirements; however, in the end, the customer is accountable for driving business value so, listen to them. Furthermore, trust in your team. If they say a component needs refactoring, they mean it. If they say it will take five days to complete a section of work, even when you only feel it should only take a day, trust them. Remember, they are experienced professionals, members of your team, and they're the ones who will be doing the work!

A Story of Influence

On one occasion, I was the Scrum Master for a team that struggled with a series of Sprints. We had committed to certain work being done but, in one particular Sprint, we missed our goals badly. In our retrospective, it surfaced that team members had grossly underestimated the complexity and scope of a series of Stories which made up the core of the Sprint.

I remember the planning meeting dynamics, but didn't recall observing a problem in the planning. When questioned, the team said that the Product Owner had influenced them to cut their estimates because of the importance *of the work. Again, I didn't remember the meeting having that sort of dynamic and pushed the team for more information. After some time, they admitted that the Product Owner had not 'made' them do anything. Based on their perception of external pressures, they had decided to be highly optimistic and only consider the sunny day paths in their estimates and subsequent work. OF COURSE, that wasn't the case and the work took much longer than expected to deliver.*

In defense of the team, this particular Product Owner had a style where he would always push his team(s) for shorter timeframes in their estimates— whether it was in Product Backlog grooming, or Sprint planning meetings. He wasn't trying to be malicious, but would always speak of the customers' desperate need for a particular feature, or mention the pressure he was getting from the CEO. There was always some sort of crisis and he would constantly let the team know about it.

Based on this behavior and his close relationship with the team, he could cause the team to totally unravel when it came to understanding, planning, collaborating and delivering good work. It turned out to be a case of good engineering vs. hacking and, much of the time, they felt influenced to "hack" in order to make their Product Owner 'happy'. Unfortunately, this wasn't the sole doing of the Product Owner. It was also part of the team dynamic and the team was certainly a partner in this dance!

Of course the trade-offs, more often than not, resulted in software issues that the Product Owner had to explain to the customers anyway. So in their efforts to do 'more', they actually did less.

In order to change this pattern, the Product Owner began to strongly emphasize the design and overall feature quality in all interactions with the team—almost always over-emphasizing its importance. Rather quickly, the team began to change the nature of its deliverables and was even able to entertain healthy quality level trade-off discussions without resorting to their prior hacking behaviors.

A Story of Strong Arming

I was recently consulting with a team on an "agile project" where they had made an entire set of up-front estimates for all features required within the project. They were part of a larger-scale Waterfall environment, so up-front requirement analysis, high level design, and schedule commitments were necessary to gain financial approval for ANY project.

Once their Director saw the estimates consolidated into the schedule, she was livid that it didn't align with business expectations. In order to ensure that the schedule was aggressive, she invited every engineer on the team into her office and went through their estimates -- line by line. In addition, she challenged them face-to-face about its length and questioned why their estimates couldn't be reduced.

To make a long story short, each engineer crumbled under the pressure. They basically agreed with whatever the Director thought were the correct estimates and then moved on. Once the entire schedule was miraculously shortened by 30%, the Director was 'happy' and the team promptly began working. Over a period of time, however, the project started to encounter problems. Since the engineers were sprinting in their deliveries, issues surfaced more quickly. However, it soon became glaringly evident that the team had underestimated the work.

A couple of problems occurred before they delivered their project. Because of schedule demands, the developers started reducing their quality practices (unit tests, pairing, FIT tests, and inspections). Instead, they put more demands on the testers to find issues in test—simply throwing it over the wall and, clearly, reverting to Waterfall behaviors.

The job also took about 35% more time, which meant that their original estimates, Waterfall, or Agile-based, closely represented their original estimates. When they finally released the product, they found (actually their customers found) many more defects than anticipated; this created even more rework time. In fact, product stability is still their primary challenge today and it all relates back to their quality vs. time decision-making.

I'm going to pick on the Director in this story. She didn't trust her team and took the wrong path of strong-arming them into reducing their estimates of the job. I've been working with software development teams for 25 years and believe this is one of the most absurd things you can do. Early on in any/every software project, things are ill defined. Engineers simply don't know the future. Anyone in a position of authority can come in and easily influence them to cut down their plans.

The results of this, however, ripple through the project and the team. It doesn't, and won't, build confidence or trust. The team doesn't self-organize. They also don't take ownership of their own incremental improvement. As a Great Product Owner, you shouldn't strong-arm or overly influence your teams. Yes, explain the business challenges. Yes, engage in healthy debate and challenge their designs, approaches, estimates, and work. But in the end, trust their craftsmanship and professionalism by not pushing too hard. If you do, they will succumb and you will _all_ lose!

Traditional Testers in Agile Teams

It's often the case that traditional testers struggle in their role transformation from Waterfall to Agile methods. In traditional teams their role is very much at the end of the pipeline. Sure, they have some early planning and preparation to do but, in the end, developers throw software "over the wall" to them for testing. Typically, the development team is over schedule and there is always compression of testing plans and time. There is also very little cross-team collaboration and often they are blamed for overall application quality—even though they play only a part in that regard.

In agile teams, the dynamic fundamentally changes. Instead of being at the end, they need to move to the beginning of the process. They actually become your partner in defining and refining User Stories. Not only in crafting the Story definitions, but where testers can really shine, is in the areas of well-formed and comprehensive acceptance tests.

Their primary and up-front role becomes, more or less, a Business Analyst one where they serve as a liaison between yourself and the development team—refining Stories and ensuring their quality. They should be partners with development, often pairing with them, to assure that feature development is clear and aligned with the customers' needs.

Another part of their role transformation surrounds that of a quality advocate or, the Voice of Quality. Many traditional testers are placed in the role of Gatekeeper, ensuring that quality goals are held within the release. However, they are rarely afforded the responsibility or time to do this effectively. In agile teams there is a holistic focus on quality, yet the team can lack some of the core experience to achieve their goals. Good testers can really help their teams here as well—by keeping their focus on up-front quality versus attempting to test it in.

In essence, agile testers move to the end of the development pipeline to become the Quality Architects within their agile teams. Their final focus is on relentless automation. Not by doing it themselves, but by influencing their entire team to automate manual tests.

The Breadth of Testing

Now that I've harped so much on your "quality mind-set", I think we ought to explore some of the dynamics of traditional testing. Testing is one of the most misunderstood aspects of solid agile development—particularly as it scales. Software testing is much more than simply unit, functional, or regression testing work. In iterative methodologies, one of the great challenges is not over or under testing; but hitting the right target of coverage given the overall changes within each iteration.

The other balancing act is to test as early as possible. For example, if you're constructing a web application, most often performance is of key concern. While you might design with performance in mind, you often simply need to test the performance dynamics of the application to fully understand everything. So, there is pressure to perform some early benchmarking and performance testing.

However, there's a Catch-22 here. Quite often you need the majority of the application to be architecturally complete before performance testing is possible or, at least, informative. This very fact can drive testing too late in the development process—or, possibly too late to do anything constructive with the feedback. Performance is just one of the testing activities that come into play. As you can see in *Figure 10*, there is a wide range of testing practices that might be required for your project.

It also illustrates the typically narrow focus of agile testing versus the breadth that is required for most projects. Plus, at the bottom, it lists some of the non-functional requirement testing activities that, again, typically extend our views towards agile testing. Clearly, agile testing is not a black box activity.

As a Great Product Owner, you need to have a firm understanding of the nuance and breadth of testing. Partner with your testers and genuinely listen to their advice regarding when, where and how much to test during your iterations. They can also provide advice for effectively planning release testing; how much testing is required, what types of testing need to be run, and in which areas of the application.

Strong Focus – Agile Team Testing	Weak Focus – Agile Team Testing
<ul><li>Unit Testing</li><li>Automated Builds – Smoke Testing</li><li>Focused – Customer Acceptance Testing</li></ul>	<ul><li>Integration Testing</li><li>Functional Testing</li><li>System Testing</li><li>Regression Testing</li><li>Performance Testing</li><li>Load Testing</li></ul>
Moderate Focus – Agile Team Testing	**Often Forgotten Testing Activities in Agile Contexts**
<ul><li>Test Driven Development (TDD)</li><li>Very limited – Integration & Regression Testing</li><li>Focused Towards Automation</li><li>Limited Exploratory Testing</li></ul>	<ul><li>Scenario Based Testing</li><li>User Acceptance Testing (UAT)</li><li>Usability Testing, Other Non-functional Testing (*see below*)</li><li>Exploratory Testing</li><li>Large-scale Automation</li></ul>
Examples of Non-Functional Testing Types	
<ul><li>Availability</li><li>Efficiency</li><li>Flexibility</li><li>Integrity</li><li>Interoperability</li><li>Maintainability</li><li>Portability</li><li>Reliability</li><li>Reusability</li><li>Robustness</li><li>Testability</li><li>Usability</li><li>Performance</li><li>Security</li></ul>	

Figure 10, Agile Testing Focus and Non-functional Testing Activities

Technical & Test Debt

One important idea the agile movement has surfaced is the notion of *technical debt*. If you've been developing software for any length of time, you've experienced technical debt; although you may not have realized there was a term coined for it. Technical debt surrounds the idea that software, virtually any software, gets more brittle over time. It ages. As different people work on it, it gets more and more complex—harder to understand, and even harder to maintain.

There are only two effective strategies for dealing with technical debt. First, is to let your software age and not really invest much in its maintenance. Over time, it becomes harder to maintain and more riddled with bugs. At some point, you get tired of the risk and you either retire the application or you decide to re-architect a replacement. In either case, you're making a Big Bang decision regarding the technical debt.

The agile methodologists have come up with a difference strategy for handling the debt. Instead of letting it accrue and get larger, what if you worked at reducing it in small steps? Suppose you try and release software with fewer bugs and then fix new bugs as soon as possible. What would happen if and when you discover a section of the code that is poorly designed, you re-design (refactor) it right then and there? This continuous improvement strategy aligns perfectly with the Agile Manifesto and is probably the better way to attack technical debt—in small, one optimization at a time, steps.

This same idea can be applied to the testing space and to both manual and automated test cases. In fact, I also think there is a notion of Technical Test Debt in most agile projects—particularly, those that can't test everything within the iteration. Whenever you move onto producing more software without performing all of your tests, you're introducing test debt in the form of untested areas of the application.

How do you compensate for this debt? As we'll explore in chapter 15, you test it out via hardening iterations that focus on integration and regression testing.

Remember

❖ Testing is not synonymous with quality. In fact, most of your quality is "baked in" well before you get to testing. Challenge your teams to adopt high quality, early development practices. Target your Sprint Goals and Done-Ness Criteria towards quality practices first.

❖ Another practice is to continuously ask your team about quality over scope and time. It's about how well they're delivering that truly makes you go faster anyway! They'll respect you for the distinction and work that much harder for you too.

❖ Technical Debt, both code and testing based, is something that most agile teams don't face as much or as well as they should. It happens quite insidiously, one day at a time. But, the effect is disabling to your teams effectiveness. Try to accommodate debt reduction work each and every Sprint. Engage your team for ideas in where and how much to perform. Create 'tension' around the need versus the business needs, but do listen and do work down your debt.

❖ Defect backlogs are another indication of Technical Debt. The same intent should apply with them. Even if they are mostly cosmetic or minor in nature, consider the cumulative effect it has on your customer and within your teams.

❖ Finally, do not overly influence your team's work estimates. If anything, emphasize the need for Solid or Good Engineering over haphazard and quick development. Quality should never be negotiated over time as it will always impact your overall efficiency…later!

Chapter 15

Release Planning and Forecasting

Great Product Owners are comfortable thinking at different levels within the context of their Backlog planning. In fact, they seem to be quite comfortable discussing the nuance of a particular feature or Story one minute and then, planning two to three releases in the future, the next. It's this sort of multi-level envisioning that is the most important aspect for this role.

That sounds like a very wide disparity of focus. How do they do it? I believe there are two keys; it's not simply that some are better than others. The first one is that the "just-in-time" nature of the Agile Methodologies frees us all for multi-level thinking, in that we don't necessarily have to create all of the details at once. We can envision, implement, and see things unfold rather than predict everything in advance. Few agile teams fully realize the freedom that this allows.

I sometimes think of it as _emergent everything_. Agile plans are really roadmaps that we adjust. So, the Product Owner is truly guiding effort _through_ their Backlog and not _by_ their Backlog.

The second key to success is empowering their entire team to be a part of the envisioning process. They need to inspire them with direction, and then wait for thoughts and ideas to emerge from the team's knowledge and progress. It's certainly not a one person show.

This also leads into forecasting as a natural extension to the planning. As the team makes progress, as any good leader, the Product Owner will adjust plans, not only towards business needs, but just as important, towards the capability and capacity of the team. This sensitivity to the team's velocity allows the Product Owner to continuously improve release *forecasting* [33] as the team gains valuable experience working together.

Variations in Tempo

One of the first things any agile team needs to establish is its own unique agile tempo. Sure, there is guidance in Scrum that 30 days (4 weeks) is the right length for a Sprint. However, that doesn't work for every team. Instead each team should discover their own best tempo with the realization that shorter is better than longer.

There's another decision regarding tempo; that is, how often will you deliver software to your customers? In many of the in-the-small agile contexts, you hear of teams delivering every Sprint. However, in many contexts, this isn't prudent or even feasible. There are a wide variety of factors that influence, what I'll refer to as your Release Tempo, for example:

- Multiple teams working on the same product codebase.
- Working across distributed teams.
- Customer(s) not able or willing to receive releases quite so frequently.
- Size of your product codebase, legacy vs. newer code, and the testing requirements.
- Regulatory or other requirements for completeness in test coverage.
- Production-like hardware limits.
- Shared environments and strong dependencies.
- Not having a fully sorted continuous Integration environment.
- General cost and budget constraints.
- Size of your team and the number of Scrum teams contributing towards the product codebase.

If you can't release every Sprint, then you'll need to create additional tempo patterns across your Sprints. These patterns usually reflect handling larger-scale work that falls outside the scope of the individual Sprint, but is also required to ready the product or project for a release point.

---

[33] Steve McConnell introduced the notion of the Cone of Uncertainty for software projects. It reflects the narrowing of estimates and improvement in forecast accuracy as we DO more work on a project and gain knowledge.

One aspect that often drives this is simply testing. Let's say, for example, you're using Scrum on a legacy codebase that has very little in the way of automated test cases currently available. Instead, it requires execution of a mostly manual test set. You have several millions lines of code and five to seven thousand manual tests. The agile tenants guide us towards testing *everything* within each Sprint. However, here that would essentially derail the entire focus of the Sprint. What do you do?

In this case, the answer is to BALANCE. Try to test as much as possible within each development Sprint. However, you won't be able to perform some types of testing, so you'll accrue some technical testing debt. After a few Sprints, and prior to a customer release, finish that testing—along with anything else that wasn't done. Surely, this isn't as Lean as it should be, and you'll need to be focusing on test automation to increase your testing coverage and speed. However, it is still better than the Waterfall.

Figure 11 illustrates, what I believe to be, the three tempos that need to be achieved in each organizations agile instance. First, there is the *development tempo*, where your team is building delivery content. Second, is the *maturation or stabilization tempo*, where they're integrating and solidifying the various work deliverables and, finally, there is your *release tempo* which is the interval that your customers can expect to see new product functionality. Clearly, all three can align, or skew, depending on the wide variety of dynamics listed earlier. The most agile view is aligned, but don't fret if you skew a bit. It's quite natural in many contexts.

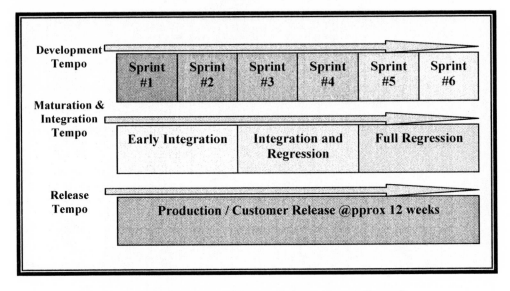

Figure 11, Development-Maturation-Release Tempo Example

The Agile Release Train

Dean Leffingwell, in his _Scaling Software Agility_ book, speaks of an Agile Release Train model that helps plan larger scale and legacy-encumbered agile teams. It's the same idea as I presented above, where you change the iteration's focus as you approach planned release points—balancing between content value and production quality readiness.

Another part of the Agile Release Train is synchronizing your Sprints. It's extremely difficult, if not impossible, to coordinate Backlogs across multiple teams if they are all Sprinting at different tempos. Instead, you want to align all of your Backlogs and Sprint Planning / Exiting activity so that everything is synchronized. This makes cross-team integration, regression testing, and release coordination much easier.

Figure 12 depicts graphically an example of a Synchronized Release Train where the teams work for two development Sprints. They focus on hardening the work by performing various forms of testing: integration, regression, and performance. Next, they work for three more development Sprints, and after that, harden again prior to a customer release point. You can clearly see the various tempos in the example. You should also get a sense for how the Backlog might look during these Sprints as the type of work evolves.

The Agile Release Train Synchronized

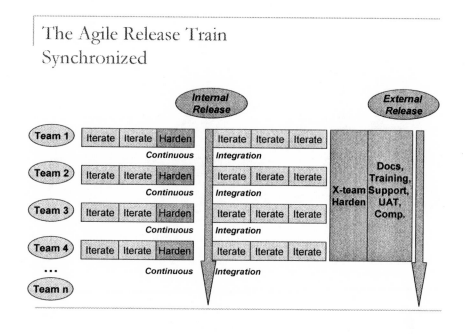

Figure 12, Example of the Agile Release Train

Figure 13 shows an alternative view for a group of teams working in a Software-as-a-Service (hosted) model. Here, the overall customer release tempo is about every 5-6 weeks. Releases need to be made on a weekend (Saturday) to avoid undue customer impact; therefore, the tempo varies with calendar alignment.

It also is a good example of how software matures by moving forward from a development environment towards a product environment. Often, environment hardware and software costs will rise as you move towards your production environment; this is another reason to shift and/or skew your focus as you target development work towards each release.

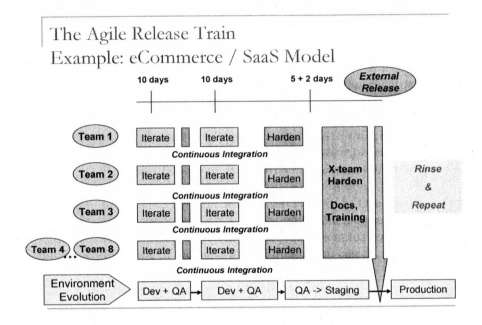

Figure 13, Example of the Agile Release Train in a SaaS Model

A Relentless Focus on Velocity

To switch gears a bit from release planning, we should also take a look at release forecasting. I think of this as being contingent on your team's velocity. All agile teams generate a velocity that is measurable. If you stay on the track that I've discussed in earlier chapters, most likely you'll be measuring it in Story Points. A personal lesson learned within a recent organizational move towards agility across several (8-10) agile teams, was that we were not *relentless in our pursuit of understanding our velocity*.

First of all, we were relatively inconsistent in our units. Some teams used Story Points in Fibonacci format, while others in High = 5, Medium = 3, Low = 1 format; a number of teams used some alternative between the two. This made it very difficult (almost impossible) for us to triangulate velocity measures across the broader development team.

Because each team had a different style, it also made it more challenging when switching teams around. Many of them had to re-learn from team-to-team and those members who were shared across several teams, found it very frustrating.

The units you choose will also influence the level of estimation. Too finely grained and you get into the weeds. Too coarse, and you miss important details that might lead you towards recomposing your Stories.

As a Great Product Owner, you play a strong part in influencing your team towards consistent units and the relentless pursuit of measuring and stabilizing their velocity. It's the one metric that you need to plan and predict release contents moving forward.

Also remember, the larger your agile organizational size, and subsequently the more individual teams you have, places even more emphasis on consistency in your velocity units. It also matters whether and how much the teams are contributing to the same codebase and singular product release train. If strongly, then I believe it becomes a critical success factor.

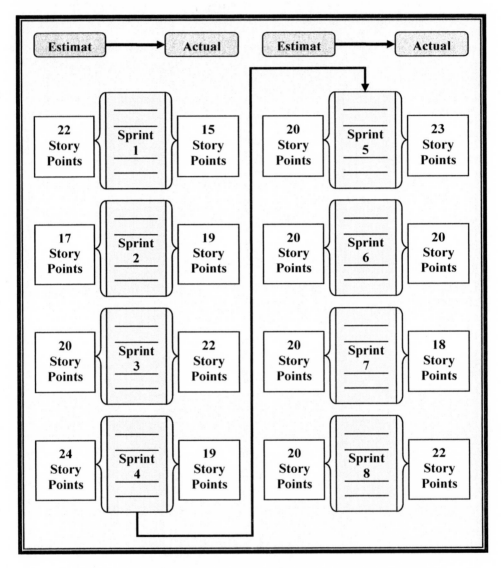

Figure 14, Rolling Velocity for Sprint-by-Sprint Forecasting Example

Velocity is Dynamic

Figure 14 illustrates a Sprint execution sequence with estimated velocity for each Sprint along with actual (output) velocity from each Sprint. In this case, I've filled in all of the iterations, but imagine if you will, that these velocity points are discovered one Sprint at a time.

Now, you enter the sequence with a large guess for team velocity -- around 22 points. In fact, you've built a release plan around that—communicating to your business stakeholders that your next release will contain 90 Story Points and, you'll deliver it in 4 2-week Sprints or, 8 weeks plus a 1-week *hardening* interval.

After the first Sprint, you know you're in a little trouble, but decide to wait for another Sprint velocity data point. After two Sprints, the team has delivered 34 Story Points worth of value. At this point you have a decision to make. Do you prefer holding to your release date? If so, you need to winnow down functionality—perhaps reprioritizing and breaking features down into *Must Haves* versus *Later Haves*.

If the feature set is imperative to your success, then you know that four Sprints weren't feasible; you'll need to convey that another Sprint is required, in other words, a 2-week slip from the original estimate.

Part of the reason for this volatility is that you had a new team with little experience surrounding their velocity for forecasting release targets. As you and the team gain experience, your ability to understand, and have more consistent velocity, will improve—as will your ability to forecast release targets. Another part of the story is that software estimation is hard, complex, and volatile. Scope must become the variable in our projects— particularly if we're trying to achieve a specific date for release!

In this case, after your initial release you'll need to forecast the next release potentially containing 150 Story Points. So, you've just completed Sprint #3 and you also need to predict the next release point as well. Given where you are, and the hints I provide above regarding your Sprint #4 through #8 performances, what would you say?

Re-forecasting Velocity

Undoubtedly, there are factors that effect velocity and you shouldn't change your release plans with every Sprint. I recommend that you average the team's velocity every 2-4 Sprints and use this as your baseline velocity for all release planning. Particularly, if you have a new team that is forming or that has gone through a recent restructuring, then you want to allow time for the velocity to stabilize and represent the normalized performance of the team.

This is another reason for trying to stick to consistent units within your teams.

Factors that Impact your Velocity

While it's a straightforward and powerful metric, velocity is also prone to instability and/or risk. That's mostly because there are so many factors that can impact its value or correctness. For example, overall team skill and keeping your team(s) together and focused are two of the critical factors for maintaining a strong and consistent velocity. Here is a list of the key factors that truly impact your velocity:

1. Team stability (retention)
2. Single vs. Multi-tasking (shared team members)
3. Team skills (Technical and Domain experience)
4. Proximity to the Product Owner
5. Co-located vs. Distributed team (multiple teams)
6. Overall team size (multiple teams)
7. Working as individuals or as a team
8. Finding creative solutions—doing less

I've listed them in loose priority order from my own experience. As a Great Product Owner, you can't simply sit by idly and hope for improved velocity within your team. Rather, work with your Scrum Master to discuss velocity as an improvement exercise within your teams. Always look for root causes as to what may be holding your teams back. Also, distinguish how you can work with each team to resolve these velocity impediments and improve their consistency and output.

Remember

❖ When working in a multiple team environment, try and stay as synchronized as possible in your Sprint dynamics. As we'll discuss in the next Chapter, use the Scrum of Scrums as a mechanism for making cross-team dependencies visible and actively managing them

❖ Backlog Sprint Planning has three basic tempos—Development, Maturation, and Release. You should be factoring all three into your planning.

❖ You need to be brutal in focusing your team on its velocity. Estimates don't really matter that much in Scrum. Rather, Sprint-over-Sprint output is your key metric for the team's ability to produce value and at what rates.

❖ When forecasting, share your estimates with the team, as well as, all release goal(s) and explain why. Put pressure on them to consistently deliver quality. Also, to deliver on their capacity to each sprint leading to the release. Adjust with them -- it's a two way street of commitment.

Chapter 16

Interactions in the Scrum of Scrums

One of the greatest gaps in the guidance that Scrum creators and pundits have provided relates to scalability. That is to say, scalability at multiple levels—across products, projects, large-scale and distributed teams, release planning, product road-maps, etc. There _is_ the nearly infamous Scrum of Scrums that has been defined. It provides guidance in very high level, loose, and amorphous terms that provide little tactical or, day-to-day help in scaling your Scrum instance.

It's basically a hierarchical view towards Scrum dynamics. Ken Schwaber, Mike Cohn, and Jeff Sutherland are some of the key Scrum thought leaders that have referenced it but, beyond a simple diagram and some hand-waving surrounding the concept, Scrum teams are pretty much left on their own when it comes to scaling. I thought it important to at least try and put some additional flavor around the concept from a Product Owner perspective, so here goes…

Scrum of Scrums

Implies that you run Scrum at _multiple levels_ in organizations where you have larger scale development. If you have multiple Scrum teams, then the Scrum Masters of those teams meet frequently, using much the same Scrum individual team dynamics to coordinate across their respective teams. You create a Meta Product Backlog for the Scrum of Scrums that drives work across the teams. There will be a Product Owner of Product Owners, call him/her the _Chief Product Owner_ for that Backlog. That there will also be a

Scrum Master of Scrum Masters, call them the *Chief Scrum Master*[34]. He or she will lead daily stand-meetings with, perhaps, slightly different questions and, on the whole, it will be Scrum—just *UP a level*. There will be a Sprint Reviews and Retrospectives that represent these aggregated team results, as well.

Mike Cohn has written *a nice article* [35] on the Scrum Alliance that explains the Scrum of Scrums dynamic. In it, he changes and extends the basic Daily Scrum questions for use in the Scrum of Scrums. Here are the questions he suggests:

1. What has your team done since we last met?
2. What will your team do before we meet again?
3. Is anything slowing your team down or getting in their way?
4. Are you about to put something in another team's way?

These questions certainly speak to broader, cross-team information sharing beyond the first level Scrum of Scrums. Therefore, you can theoretically scale it upwards for any sized organization. While conceptually this sounds easy; it is, of course, the way you would scale any larger scale software work. The devil, as they say, is in the details of how to implement it within *your* organizational context.

This is where most of the traditional Scrum guidance stops—leaving implementation to each organization. The point is that every organization, beyond the small team agile sweet spot, has some need for Scrum of Scrum dynamics. They need to define, create, and then, refine it for themselves.

From a Product Owner perspective, I've seen multiple levels of defined Scrum of Scrums that you may want to participate in, and possibly contribute to, later on. *Figure 15* is an example of the layering that I've found to be typical in larger scale Scrum instances.

---

[34] To the best of my knowledge, there isn't agreement within the Scrum community as to what to call these second level or beyond Product Owners and Scrum Masters. I've heard 'Chief' used as well as 'Meta' in some contexts. I'm sure there are others…

[35] http://www.scrumalliance.org/articles/46-advice-on-conducting-the-scrum-of-scrums-meeting

More often than not, the layers and the focus points are strongly influenced by several key factors such as:

- The overall size of the development organization.
- The number of Enterprise-level products being deployed, as well as, product lines being supported.
- The number of individual Scrum teams contributing (in parallel) to each of the primary product lines.
- The integration requirements across the separate products (examples: look and feel, data consistency and sharing, regulatory guidelines and consistent functional compliance testing).
- The existence of a PMO function and the negotiated requirements they have for integration.

It's Not CMMi or a Formal Organizational Structure!

Don't think of these layers in the same way you might as an organizational structure or CMMi implementation. That would be a mistake. Instead, I like to emphasize their need by illuminating the conversations that naturally happen within larger scale Scrum instances. These conversations occur at different levels. For example, Scrum of Scrum conversations usually surround integration and dependency collaboration amongst multiple teams working together on an individual product or project.

Scrum of Scrum of Scrums are at the next higher level of communication. Again, multiple teams are implied, and the conversations surround resource sharing, dependencies, code and component integration and system testing, along with product deployment. Often release planning is a part of the conversation—as is budgeting and metrics for the projects.

Just as an example, I'm basing the structure in *Figure 15* on a hypothetical organization where there are three separate products integrated into a SaaS (Software as a Service) framework, with each succinct product having multiple (three-six) Scrum teams contributing application code to each.

Given these characteristics, then a Scrum of Scrums framework along the following lines _might be_ a useful way to integrate Scrum deliverables and target them towards your customers—

Individual Scrum Team – Level 1 or (S1)

Conversations surrounding – Team specific work, progress, impediments, and dependencies

General Focus of Activities	(Chief) and Product Owner Engagement
1'st level tier, focused towards product development; driving production of high value software components / projects from the individual teams.	Individual Product Owner for each team; defining and driving Backlog of work. Traditional PO role responsibilities.

Scrum of Scrums – Level 2 or (S2)

Conversations surrounding – Cross-team Code Integration and Testing, Dependency Management, Release Point Coordination, Cross-Team Backlog Management

General Focus of Activities	(Chief) and Product Owner Engagement
2'nd level tier, focused towards cross-team collaboration, Sprint results integration, and coordination towards the next product release point. Close to the same dynamics as the Scrum teams—Meta Backlog, Scrum Master, frequent / daily meetings, Sprint Planning, Review, etc. During times of release preparation, cross-team repair interactions and testing interactions occur for full coverage integration, regression and other forms of testing.	Setup release plan so that the individual teams understand dependencies and expectation surrounding all work (integration, resource sharing, testing, deployment) leading towards the release. Helping teams to manage cross-Backlog dependencies and deliverables. Resolving conflicts and issues. Attending daily Scrum of Scrums stand-up during release intervals.

Figure 15a, Example of Hierarchical Scrum of Scrum PO Responsibilities

Scrum of Scrums of Scrums – Level 3 or (S3)

Conversations surrounding – Resource Utilization and Dependencies, Overall Release Dynamics, and Budgeting and Forecasting, Risks, Metrics

General Focus of Activities	(Chief) and Product Owner Engagement
3'rd level tier, intended to focus on staffing, resource sharing, product portfolio management, ROI, etc. from the various projects. Can also drive cross product line consistency, for example, look and feel, quality levels, and regulatory and security requirements. Often drives budgeting and overall Product Portfolio planning across a particular larger scale or enterprise-level product or product family.	Business case development, phase-gate control for beginning projects. Portfolio planning leading towards effective resource utilization and balancing. Defining overall product/project consistency goals—usability, quality, security, regulatory / certification, etc. Running planned Alpha/Beta programs. Overall committed release plans and external coordination within cross-functional teams.

Scrum of Scrums of Scrums of Scrums – Level 4 or (S4)

Conversations surrounding – Scrum Process and Adoption Strategy

General Focus of Activities	(Chief) and Product Owner Engagement
4'th level tier, in my experience tending to focus towards Scrum and Agile adoption strategies and training across the entire organization. Leading in defining 'standards' or guard rails for cross-team Scrum utilization. Perhaps including focus groups for Scrum Masters and Product Owners.	Chief Product Owner is fully engaged here at a leadership level focusing on goal setting, integrating road-maps into Backlogs, and driving coordinated deliverables. Effective staffing and training strategies of Product Owners are also defined here.

Figure 15b, Example of Hierarchical Scrum of Scrum PO Responsibilities

A "Scrum of Scrums" Story

A short time ago, I had a development organization in St. Petersburg, Russia that was split up in two scrum teams to work on a couple of products. These products were very different in functionality, but shared a common UI, data storage, and communication layer. The teams shared a Test manager, a Research and Development manager / Scrum Master, a Business Analyst, and the Product Owner. The majority of the other team members were assigned to one of the two teams.

A few of them were assigned to a team on a release basis (4 Sprints) or a Sprint basis depending on the technology affected by the release or the focus of the Sprint. For example, Sprint #4 was typically focused on getting the product ready for release to one (or multiple) customer(s). This Sprint, therefore, always had more testers than other Sprints.

We would skew the releases and Sprints so that we would have the maximum amount of time between Sprint end/beginning and the same for the releases. This way, we could shift people for specific Sprints with minimal impact on the other project. We were also able to focus better on the needs of a specific team. The Product Owner, the Scrum Master, and the Business Analyst would participate in Product demos, Sprint reviews, and Sprint planning for both products.

We had daily stand- up meetings where the entire team would participate, as well as, weekly meetings to discuss the integration of technology and plans with the Scrum Master, test manager, and architects. In this meeting, we would make decisions regarding higher level architectural or strategic directions. In general, these were things that would either not affect the team in the next couple of Sprints, or, they would affect both teams equally.

We (the Product Owner, Scrum Master, and sometimes the business analyst or architect) additionally had regular meetings where we would discuss process optimizations, technology needs, and/or lessons learned. These meetings were held on a regular basis, but without a scheduled time. Most meetings were scheduled whenever there was a need – usually, every 2-4 weeks. Follow up meetings were planned to work out details and tracking changes to ensure that all changes were a step forward, rather then a step backward.

Furthermore, we had quarterly planning meetings with representatives of Sales and Marketing, as well as the executive team to track our progress, refine plans and to adapt to changed business needs. This was the time to get a formal "thumbs up" stating that we were still on the right track (or, if not, to change accordingly).

Having thought about this more, I realize I was having four levels of Scrum of Scrums :-). It just never felt as structured or rigid as it seemed on paper...

—Michael Faisst

I like Michael's story because it emphasizes the collaborative looseness and application of common sense that needs to be an integral part of your Scrum of Scrums definition. It also helps illustrate the different types of conversation and collaboration that are needed.

Architectural Coordination

Another important part of the Scrum of Scrum's discussion is technical and cross-team coordination. I think Great Product Owners push their Backlogs, and subsequently their teams, towards the relentless pursuit of zero dependencies.

The complimentary force to this is that most developers push towards greater dependencies. They're more comfortable with larger scale features developed "in-the-large", that require greater cohesion. I get the sense this comes from our traditional training and experience in how to build software architectures. In your role, you should constantly challenge teams to break things down. But, more important than that, to try and break things down into component parts that have loose or little dependencies.

There's a wonderful *blog entry* [36]by Mike Cottmeyer, of VersionOne, that speaks to dependencies as being one of the key inhibitors to enterprise level agile scaling. In a nutshell, he alludes to successful agile scalability being directly tied to the organization's ability to create products, features, stories, components, tasks, etc. that are decoupled from one another. In other words, minimization of dependencies; thus, enabling each small Scrum team to be able to deliver value on their own right and not encumbered by the work of other teams.

---

[36] http://blog.versionone.net/blog/2008/12/the-secret-to-organizational-agility.html

When you do have dependencies, then the Scrum of Scrums structure is a good way to make them visible across various teams that are trying to manage them. Next, we'll explore a few strategies for collaborating when you do have dependencies. Trust me you will...

Visiting Pigs

One practical approach I've seen work in handling cross-team dependencies being driven from the Scrum of Scrums, is to foster dependency team membership by including team members as _visiting Pigs_ in other Scrum teams. When two teams have a clear dependency, then one team sends a 'visitor' to the other team's Sprint Planning and Daily Stand-up meetings to ensure representation and, maintain continuity.

Quite often, these visitors have an architectural view, or slant, within the team—so they're more or less, ensuring that work meets higher level architectural goals and/or standards. Nonetheless, this is an effective way to make cross-team dependencies visible so that both teams can properly handle them.

Story – Another Approach

I worked at an eCommerce company where we had approximately 8-10 Scrum teams running in parallel on 3 separate product lines of a SaaS offering. Architectural coordination was one of the things we struggled with quite a bit.

Initially, we had separate architectural groups that were tasked with providing architectural guidance across all of the teams. We noticed, however, that since the architects didn't operate within a working Scrum team, their ideas had a "throw it over the wall" flavor to them, which didn't sit well with the teams. In spite of this, they did need time to consider system level architectural designs independent of all other activities.

We all hit on a compromise that seemed to work quite well.

The architects (UI / Usability, Middleware and Database) would attend all of the Sprint Planning sessions across our (8-10) teams—looking for opportunities where they were needed or could engage in the Sprint work. They would sign-up for work at a 50% utilization level based on their perceptions of cross-team dependencies, needs, and opportunity.

This arrangement provided some real 'glue' between our teams at the discrete technology level that we didn't have before implementing it. Because it was self-directed and adaptive to what our overall Meta Product Backlog required, the results were better than we had when we were more prescriptive in assigning our architects to teams.

Remember

❖ You'd be surprised how often even relatively small organizations need Scrum of Scrum dynamics installed. Don't think of it as process overhead. Instead, it's the guiding force for integrating Scrum as you grow your teams or install Scrum in larger organizational contexts. Define it early and then evolve it.

❖ I emphasize conversation and collaboration as the drivers behind Scrum of Scrum installation. My 'layers' above try and focus you on the different types of conversations and collaborations that are needed. Don't get 'stuck' by the layering

❖ Scrum of Scrums is also the 'glue' that provides a connection to your cross-functional interactions. For example, if you need to collaborate with your PMO or an external vendor for schedule commitments, then the Scrum of Scrum makes the interaction need and actions visible. It also can provide architectural cohesion as the story illustrated.

Chapter 17

Organizational Dynamics of Scaling

Agility, when first introduced in the guise of Scrum and Extreme Programming, was very much a small context play with small co-located teams of less than ten engineers. They worked directly with customers or their advocates and utilized heavy face-to-face collaboration. In addition, they displayed a strong focus on the in-the-small, quality-centric, development practices.

They also developed important applications, typically not at the Enterprise-level, or for real-time safety critical applications, or large-scale and regulated applications; that just wasn't the sweet spot for those methods. However, web applications were definitely an area of strength because of their UI-centric nature where the customer really did need to continuously engage in their evolution.

Since Agile Methods were not a prescriptive process, but a learned and adaptive one, there was (and is) very little in the way of guidance. You really had to gather some information by initial reading or training to gain your real *agile chops* by raw experience. Again, that works well in small teams.

However, as agility begins to become a more mainstream methodology, it is encountering more and more situations that are outside of its core context or sweet spot. While these methods can and do adapt quite well, it takes additional work, energy, and effort to do so successfully. It also requires a person to adapt to methods beyond their simple natures and, potentially, *stretch* them towards the more traditional approaches they're intended to replace. Or, at the very least, learn to interface with those more traditional approaches.

Therefore, this chapter is for the Great Product Owner who is working in contexts outside the scope of _small agility_. I'll try to touch on specific areas where you'll need to make adjustments; only be aware of additional challenges in order to increase your effectiveness.

Scaling the Product Owner Organization

If operating as a Product Owner in a team is broad and challenging (and it is), what does it feel like when you have multiple teams contributing software towards the same product or application? Imagine that there are eight independent Backlogs and eight independent Product Owners driving towards the same product goal, but in an uncoordinated fashion.

Sounds like chaos to me!   How about you?

To effectively integrate the team's work, there needs to be a common Backlog which captures all tasks that the teams will be focusing on. It actually speaks to features, but also to relationships, dependencies, and boundaries for the entire project. It represents this so that teams can take on individual streams of related work, but at the same time, there is cohesion and consistent integration direction and workflows towards a larger, more integrated, customer deliverable.

Scrum recommends a separate Backlog and a Product Owner for each team. However, how do you manage consistency, coordination, and collaboration across each of the teams? The Scrum of Scrums doesn't help in defining a Meta Product Backlog which is the product development strategy that will be executed across all eight of those teams.

Instead, this challenge falls squarely on the shoulders of the Product Owners, albeit at a different level—the Product and Road-Map levels. Usually, in larger scale agile instances, there is a Product Level organization that includes multiple Product Owners. More often than not, a Chief Product Owner will lead this group and be responsible for broad product feature sets, delivery road-maps, commitments to delivery time-frames, and overall product consistency and achievement of quality targets.

It's this Chief Product Owner who creates and maintains that higher level Meta Product Backlog that drives individual team Product Backlogs and, subsequently, the Scrum teams. They're also responsible for scaling and growing the Product Owner—leading to cross Backlog and cross Product Owner interactions and participation within the Scrum of Scrums structure.

Many agile organizations fail to scale their agile instances at the product level as much as they do at the engineering team level. They simply miss the need for it—thinking that a disparate group of Product Owners should be able to "work amongst themselves" to integrate the work. While this can work in the small, it doesn't scale well. I'd also argue that these larger scale organizations know very well how to operate with larger product planning and coordination, they just think agility takes them off the hook for the work—which is totally untrue.

Implications of the PMO

When I think of Traditional PMO (Project Management Office) structures, I think of Scrum of Scrum-like characteristics at the Project Management level. Of course, in larger scale organizations—not just in size or distributed natures, but those organizations who carry out many distinct projects. In these cases, the PMO is trying to evaluate, understand, coordinate, and close on a broad portfolio of projects within the organization. Resource utilization is usually a big part of their role, both for human and capital equipment.

If I were to make a generic list to represent their key focus points, it might include much of the following:

- Project business case development, in conjunction with the Product Manager and/or Product Owner organizations, and driving the approval decision-making process.
- Prioritization, resource staffing, and scheduling of 'approved' projects.
- Resource and cost / budget management and tracking.
- Project execution tracking, risk management, and metrics.
- Project governance and project close-out.

All of these are aggregated under a banner of portfolio management. The priority is less about the individual projects at this level, and more about effective execution of a suite of projects that are driving business value, resource utilization efficiency, cost management, and driving innovation.

Depending on your level of PMO definition, there is almost a direct mapping between Scrum of Scrums levels two and three (in *Figure 15*) towards the PMO. In fact, your Scrum of Scrums definition, and the role of the Chief Product Owner and Product Owners within it, will heavily depend upon your PMO organizational definition and processes.

The Development organization, Scrum organization, Product organization, and the PMO need to work together to effectively define these relationships. In many cases, the resulting processes or dynamics will *stretch* your Scrum agility. While your challenge will be to stretch, retain as much of your core agile tenants and core agile behaviors as possible.

Chief Product Owner – Office of the Product Owner

In the last Chapter we explored scaling the organization and the role of Scrum of Scrums. In this chapter, we will touch on what role the Chief Product Owner plays in effectively scaling the Product Owner organization. Also, to create one that can support the growing instance of Scrum being used for product development.

A large part of that scaling isn't simply collaborating with the Scrum of Scrums and feeding the teams a Backlog. Instead, it surrounds creating a Product Owner organization that has the depth, breadth, and skills required to support their agile teams, while *still* supporting traditional Product Management responsibilities.

One mechanism to help do this would be to create an *Office of the Product Owner* which somewhat mirrors the PMO and Scrum of Scrums, but from a pure product perspective. This would be the function and team that would support all aspects of instantiating agility within your product teams. This is where you'd take a hard look at individual capabilities and decide how you can, and should, support the agile team requirements—with single Product Owners, or combinations of individuals, that meet the skill-set requirements.

It's also the function where you build an effective organization of Product Ownership—regardless of how many individual Product Owners and/or Product Managers you need. As an example, I've seen Product Owner organizations hire traditional Business Analysts to fill the skills-set and team needs for User Stories and other forms of requirements. They've even brought User Experience skills to help define more useable systems.

It's the Chief Product Owners responsibility to develop their organization to effectively meet all of the external Marketing demands and the internal Agile demands.

Dealing with Other Methodologies

As an Agile Coach, I often get the question—how do you handle agile interactions with traditional waterfall oriented teams? To be honest, I usually try and steer the questioner away from these interactions by asking them to find another project opportunity for agile adoption or use. The simple truth is that these interactions are difficult at best, and often impossible to balance the traditional vs. agile execution differences.

For example, let's say that you're an agile shop that has some serious experience and success using these methods. Then, your company is acquired by another one that uses more traditional, staid development methods. They are clearly the _parent_ when it comes to approaches and, while they might superficially support your agile approaches, they'll inevitably want you to integrate with them and "do it their way".

Let's look at this a bit closer. For example, if you're exchanging requirements with one of their teams, they'll want those requirements entirely defined up-front and in fine detail. They'll want them signed-off and kept under relatively tight change control. Clearly, as an agile team you'll be constrained by this. In fact, it will probably create a great deal of contention as you try to allow your requirements to emerge with the project and still meet their requests for defined and refined requirements.

The more you meet expectations, the more you'll be limiting your emergent practices and falling back into a Waterfall-esque mindset. This same sort of trade-off will pervade many of your other interactions and reduce, or negate, your overall agile effectiveness.

The Project Triangle – Triple Constraint

Another distinctive area of contention will be project planning. Your parent organization will probably want a holistic, end-to-end, project plan for each of your projects. These are intended to document fixed scope, fixed cost, and fixed schedule targets for each effort. While agile projects endeavor to align with more traditional views, the key variable in traditional software projects is quality, while the key variable in agile projects is scope (as can be seen in *Figure 16)*.

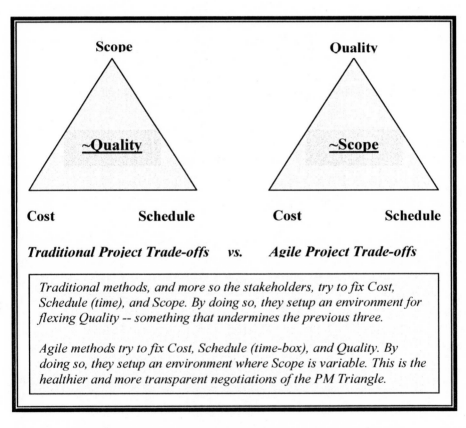

Traditional methods, and more so the stakeholders, try to fix Cost, Schedule (time), and Scope. By doing so, they setup an environment for flexing Quality -- something that undermines the previous three.

Agile methods try to fix Cost, Schedule (time-box), and Quality. By doing so, they setup an environment where Scope is variable. This is the healthier and more transparent negotiations of the PM Triangle.

Figure 16, Traditional vs. Agile Project Constraint trade-offs

From a business perspective, this adjustment has profound implications. For years, traditional projects have varied their quality practices because of constraint pressures. This has lulled those stakeholders into behaviors surrounding demands for more and more features with fixed costs and schedules. Yet, along the way, they have never had to directly acknowledge or face the quality trade-offs (bugs, rework, miss implemented features, lack of cohesive architecture, stale documentation, etc.) that this behavior creates within their teams.

The question of Requirement Artifacts

One of the common perceptions surrounding agility is that it's documentation-light—particularly in the area of requirements. That's essentially true, but mostly driven from the needs within smaller team and project contexts. In a far more broad set of contexts, agile teams actually need to increase their requirements and other artifacts, both in size and in earlier development, which places very traditional requirement writing pressure on the Product Owner and on the team. What are some of those contexts?

Large teams; Distributed teams: As teams scale, face-to-face communication and collaboration breaks down in its effectiveness and feasibility. You simply can't be as effective and there are too many communication channels.

Volatile Teams: In these cases I'm speaking of attrition, either by *M&A activity*[37], growth and/or true attrition based on market conditions. The truth is, if you have high turnover in your agile teams, you need to have more artifacts to capture product and project intellectual capital for future team members to use in understanding your systems.

Outsourced activities or dealing with Third Parties: Again, you just can't expect other teams to come and interact with your teams to gain system knowledge. It's much harder to setup contracts for this approach and hold external firms accountable. Instead, you must define more traditional Statements of Work and Measurable Outcomes in order to allow the successful execution of external work.

Regulatory or Process Requirements: Traceability is often required in many organizations or product domains. It entails tracing requirements to code and executed test cases, verifying that you've implemented and tested

---

[37] Mergers and acquisitions

what your requirement set. In these environments, you'll need extra rigor when defining and tracking your requirements and tests.

The above are just a few of the contexts where you need to adjust your agile artifact definition levels. There are many others. The point is that you should be flexible in your requirement writing, but don't be fooled into thinking that meeting your context expectations as being bad or un-agile.

Instead, look to be lean in all of your artifacts. Deliver them in pieces -- Just-Enough and Just-in-Time, to all of your internal partners. Instead of _pushing_ work towards them, wait for them to ask for, or _pull it,_ from you. That way you always deliver just what is required—and nothing more.

Story of a Distributed Team Interaction

Switching gears a bit, I thought it would be useful to share a story of one Product Owner's solution to collaborating with a remote development team.

In my last SCRUM experience I ran a software development team in St. Petersburg while I was in Florida. This level of distribution brought some interesting challenges to both planning and day- to-day operations. Given the time difference, I was not always readily available when the team had questions. Planning sessions had to be shortened because these intense meetings can become increasingly harder as time differences cut down on the available time window. Language differences and sound quality also made these meetings difficult to participate in.

At this point, I had decided to have a liaison on the team in the position of Product Analyst. This helped a tremendous amount as this person was available to do more leg work regarding meeting preparations and grooming the back-log, Beyond that, they helped with having a local contact that team members could talk to for clarification on specific items (since this individual had done much research on the topics that I deemed important).

However, some challenges remained. We ended up with more meetings to cover issues that had already been covered in the team's daily scrum. Mainly, because my proxy couldn't resolve the issue, or the team felt they had to explain the implications of a decision to me personally. For a while, *we tried daily scrums at the end of their days yet, that seemed less productive because of the timing and requirements to discuss all topics in English, rather then just those topics that required my direct participation.*

All in all, however, I wouldn't do distributed SCRUM without having, at least, a liaison of the Product Owner close to the development organization.

—Michael Faisst

Distributed Teams – Tooling

There's a clear dilemma in the agile space when it comes to tooling. As the Agile Manifesto states, we'd like to emphasize *Individuals and Interactions over Process and Tools*. Many of the agile pundits, *Ron Jeffries* [38] among them, go out of their way to emphasize this point when questions regarding tools come about.

The point is that tools can often get in the way of achieving proper agile team behavior. Teams can simply follow, or trust the tools to tell them what to do while doing less collaboration. I've seen this occur quite often in my coaching practice. It doesn't help that the IT world, in general, has a tendency to *throw tools* at new methods and problems with the false hope that they'll solve everything.

At the same time, tools are a godsend when it comes to distributed team collaboration and planning within Scrum. The balance is to start early on with simple, low-fidelity cards and wall oriented planning. Perhaps, bring in some web based collaboration (Wiki's) along with Microsoft Excel. That way the team has some distributed support, but isn't leaning too heavily on those tools.

---

[38] I've lurked on the *Scrum development* yahoo list for quite a few years and watched as Ron consistently and pointedly challenged folks on tools. His persistence in always trying to drive the thinking towards the simplest tool sets, while encouraging basic agile tenants, is not only admirable but in my view absolutely right.

Once you've got some experience and maturity in agile collaboration, begin looking at some of the more distributed solutions for agile tooling. There's a short list of tools that might prove helpful in these cases and, in no particular order, they include:

- Rally
- VersionOne
- Microsoft TFS
- ScrumWorks
- Jira + Greenhopper

My advice here would be to not lead with tools, but to plan for a tool-set once you start instantiating Scrum across your larger and distributed teams. I'd also advise you to have a quarterly checkpoint of sorts, call it an assessment, where you examine the behavior of your teams relative to your tools usage. This will ensure that you haven't become overly dependent on these tools and that they're simply still an adjunct for your Scrum teams.

Connections to Your Stakeholders

It's fairly easy to maintain your transparency and connectedness to your stakeholders in small instances of agility. Keeping your stakeholders effectively engaged at scale can be much tougher.

We spoke about one aspect of that engagement earlier in this guide— surrounding the importance of getting key stakeholders to attend your Sprint Reviews. In the larger context case, that probably means you're conducting remote or distributed reviews. While it might be daunting to schedule or set these up, broad inclusion becomes even more important at scale.

Leverage distributed meeting technology to display your review for remote attendees. Make sure you give early enough notice so all can attend. Most importantly, make it clear as to what you're delivering and why (from a value perspective). Generate some excitement to get their attention and attendance.

If you know a key stakeholder is busy, reach out to them and ask for a delegate. Or, send them a recording or minutes following the review so they can clearly understand what went on. In a larger scale, maintain effective customer connectivity

Distributed Stand-ups

To take this idea a step further, please try and make your other Scrum meetings highly accessible. For example, setup a conference call for folks to listen in to your Daily Scrum as Chickens. Occasionally, use a video link for Daily Scrums and Sprint Planning meetings. You'll receive a positive return for any effort you make to simulate small team agile behavior for larger, more broadly distributed teams.

Borrowing an 'Old' Idea

In traditional project planning, there's the notion of a communications plan where a Project Manager will define roles and responsibilities for effectively communicating project state across the team and around to stakeholders. You do this as part of project chartering—so very early in the project.

What's useful about the technique is that you define your key communications channels (people, needs, methods) early, and establish a communications commitment on the part of your team members and key stakeholders. While it's not perfect, it may help you to connect to your stakeholders—particularly if they're accustomed to the technique.

Remember

❖ While I don't have a silver bullet solution, I see a very common pattern where Product Owner organizations lag all others in agile organizational adoption. Since they're so crucial, the reverse should be the standard. I can't emphasize enough the need for a Chief Product Owner and Meta-Backlogs when you start to scale.

❖ No matter how many different methodologies or PMO structures you deal with, try to maintain your agile Scope trade-off dynamics and don't allow Quality to be compromised instead. You'll go slower of you do!

❖ It will be tempting to simply *throw tools* at your agile scaling challenges. While they play a part in it, don't lose your agile basics for collaboration and communication.

Chapter 18

Wrapping Up

Here's the _Elevator Pitch_ for this guide—

1. Engage your team—sit with them, share challenges with them, work with them and always be honest
2. Be a true Servant Leader within your team; lead by example in collaboration with the Scrum Master
3. Set forth clear Goals at all levels. They shouldn't be easy or impossible goals, but something excitingly in between.
4. Appropriately manage your Backlog. Consider your role as the facilitator of it. Encouraging everyone to contribute to it and own its execution.
5. Be balanced in your Backlog—considering not just features and business value, but the broad nuance surrounding building great software.
6. The most important part of User Stories is Collaboration. Don't refine them too early. Let them foster ambiguity—leading your team to figure things out.
7. Trust your team; Listen to them. Understand their strengths, weaknesses, and capabilities.
8. You can achieve much better than Waterfall performance in your release forecasting. Just focus on velocity and maintain consistency in your teams—learning and leveraging their capacity.
9. Remember the breadth aspects of being a Great Product Owner. If you can't do it all, raise it up as an impediment and look / expect help. You and your team deserve it.
10. Did I say—Trust your Team?

Agile 'Speed'

There's a common perception on the part of many organizations that the Agile Methodologies, including Scrum, deliver software faster. That they are a SPEED play when it comes to software development!

No, you say! Nobody is naïve enough to believe that. Everyone truly Grok's the Zen of Agility and understands it's value proposition.

Perhaps, I've been living under a rock, or working in the wrong environments, but I've encountered way too many people who don't seem to 'get' agility; I want to share on a final, but what I feel is a very important point.

Agile is NOT faster in ALL contexts!

In fact, I encountered a client who was using Scrum across the board, but in reality it was only Agile in their software development teams and traditional Waterfall in their testing teams. Do you know what? They noticed that throughput was actually 1.5 times slower in this model than it was in pure Waterfall. The point being that even Agile done poorly can actually be incredibly painful, disruptive, and slower than Waterfall.

So, what are the key focus points to drive agile speed? There are three that come to mind?

1. **It's about up-front quality**—or avoiding rework. Rework is the great enemy of moving quickly! It's about gaining feedback on what works, what doesn't work, and making changes early, quickly, and in the small.

2. **It's about minimizing what you do**—so simplicity in everything; avoidance of Gold Plating, applying the Pareto Principle (80:20 Rule) to your feature sets, working on the highest priority items, becomes the team's Prime Directive.

3. **It's about activating the creativity of your team**—instead of your team following plans or User Stories give them true insight into the customers' needs and foster an environment where they can solve those problems using their innovation and creative abilities.

As a Great Product Owner, please focus on the role you can play influencing these three points within your own and teams work. It will make a HUGE difference!

Product Owners Rock!

If I haven't said it before in the text, I want to go on record now. I don't like the *Single Wring-able Neck* analogy. Instead I'd like to change it to the Most Rockin' Role of Scrum. Great Product Owners are a central character in the success of Scrum, the job is tough and the good ones are certainly skilled professionals. So, endeavor to be a Great One, trust and depend on your teams, and Rock On!

Feedback

My hope is that this short guide provided some valuable insights and ideas on how you might become a Great Product Owner. However, it was never intended to be exhaustive or prescriptive in nature. If you've learned one thing in your agile experience and reading, the learning primarily comes in the *doing*.

If in your *doing* you find things you want to add or change in the text, please send them to me. While I intend to keep it pragmatic, short, and approachable, I'd enjoy hearing your experiences, changes, comments, ideas, virtually anything from the agile community that might improve this guide. My driving intention in writing this was to help, so if I can inspect and adapt towards improvement…that's the point.

Please send all such commentary to: bob@rgalen.com. You can also connect with me via LinkedIn http://www.linkedin.com/in/bobgalen if you wish to stay in touch and network via that mechanism.

Cheers!
Bob.

Appendix A

10 Product Owners Myths

Simply a work-in-progress, but might lead to something useful…

1. **They're not a member of the team**

2. **They never have enough time**

3. **Business value is the only determinant of priority**

4. **They know everything the customer needs or wants**

5. **They're the only one contributing to the Product Backlog**

6. **The have to be full-time**

7. **There can be only one**

8. **It's always the Product Manager**

9. **They make technical decisions or tell the team how to approach their work**

10. **They don't do Sprint work**

Appendix B

Project Chartering as a Means of Starting Scrum Projects

What is it?

It's a *Process* and *Artifacts* that—

- ✓ Establishes the vision state for the project
- ✓ Defines key goals and requirements
- ✓ Captures and sets customer expectations
- ✓ Defines project participants and their roles
- ✓ Defines limits and constraints
- ✓ Establishes all resource needs and overall cost targets
- ✓ Creates a high level view to the WBS and schedule
- ✓ Initiates negotiation and tradeoffs
- ✓ Ultimately defines success

Another view—

A charter is a central document or a set of supporting documents that defines the purpose, nature and characteristics of an about to be undertaken software project.

It is typically constructed early in the project lifecycle, hopefully before the project is staffed and the business is pushing for a delivery date. It is usually created collaboratively as a team and shared with stakeholders upon completion.

It is intended to clearly set the stage for the project—aligning the team and setting goals and expectations.

It's often the case that a Charter leads to an early project approval 'Gate' as part of an organizational project approval life-cycle phase. Usually the keys to the approval involve Cost, Schedule, and Scope—so very much of a fixed price contractual view.

Components of an Effective Project Charter

Charter Element	Focus
Purpose	Primary rationale, compelling and clear, mission and vision for the effort
Goals	Technical, business, product, and team objectives
Scope	Customer needs, functional and non-functional requirements, bounds
Organization	Executive / stakeholder, project, functional organization structures
Resources	Space, equipment, people, skill sets and capabilities, collaboration support, tools
Approaches	Strategy, methodologies, processes, tools, and techniques
Priorities	Ordering, importance, trade-offs, relative to other projects
Assumptions and Constraints	Restrictions, limits, bounds – team, process, product, and schedule
Risks	Top 'n' risks, known, previous history, uncertainty elaborated, with mitigation plans
Sign-off	Stakeholder approval; contract nature

Appendix C

Quick Diversion into LEAN Software Development

Throughout the guide, I've made references to lean practices. I thought it would be useful here to highlight a few of the *thinking patterns* surrounding *LEAN software development*[39]:

- **Avoid Waste:** Waste in this sense is doing anything within a software project that doesn't equate to real business VALUE. Now, this isn't avoiding quality work, but it is focused towards limiting Gold Plating across your entire work spectrum. The Product Owner must see value in the work! And agree to pay for it.

- **Avoid Multi-tasking:** Try to work on one thing at a time. First, your focus will be better, which will drive up quality. Second, you'll save time as multi-tasking has a task-switch penalty of 20% or more. If you do switch, only do so when your first priority is *Blocked*, then switch back when it's *Clear*.

- **Work on Small Chunks**: The smaller your units of work (Features, Stories, Work Tasks), the better off you are. You can (and should) drive them to DONE as quickly as possible, putting that work behind you.

- **As a Team, Work on a FEW Things at a Time:** Is it better to work on many things or a few things at one time from a queuing theory perspective? The answer is a few things and they should be relatively small. Focus on getting them DONE and then move onto more.

- **Generate High Degrees of Collaboration**: It's much better to have small groups of your team working together than sets of individuals working alone and integrating their work later.

---

[39] And of course the books by Mary and Tom Poppendieck are the clear leaders in this space. If you're interested in Lean, they're must reads...

- **Trust the Professionalism of your Team**: Much of our process definition and work limits are based on a fundamental distrust of our teams. Turn that around and expect them to be professionals, do professional (high quality) work, and to deliver results.

- **Deliver Results Quickly, Get Feedback**: This is a pervasive point and why there's a Daily Scrum, Sprint Review, and a reason your team needs your daily engagement.

- **Deliver Just-Enough**: Don't be presumptuous that you know _exactly_ what is _minimally required_ from your customer. Deliver something _small_ and allow your customer to PULL more from you as it's needed. It's this strategy that achieves Just-Enough

- **Deliver Just–in–Time:** Waiting until just the right moment to deliver has great advantages; you've maximized your feedback and continued learning which lead up to that delivery. Often that learning will lead to higher quality and more efficient designs and solutions to your customers' challenges.

- **PULL over PUSH:** Always leverage a pull from your customers (internal and external) to drive your delivery priority instead of trying to anticipate their needs by pushing delivery to them.

- **Be a Professional; Act with Integrity:** In many cases in teams, I've heard engineers blame their supervisors or management for their doing a poor job of design, coding or testing. While they certainly influence engineer behavior, we all must remain professionals and stay committed to delivering quality work. Regardless of pressures.

7 Wastes in Software Development

Waste	Description
1. Partially Done Work	While work is partially complete, it has no value. Think of a car in-process, it only achieves its value when it's 100% complete and can be placed in inventory for sale.
2. Extra features	Avoid "Gold Plating" in its many forms. The most obvious is adding features that really aren't required. However, it pervades all aspects of software—design, documentation, planning, architecture, etc.
3. Relearning	Related to handing work off to others in a queue. Each time another team member has to "pick up" the work, they need to go through a re-learning of what's been done before them.
4. Handoffs	Strongly related to relearning, the physical number of hand-offs before achieving Done or 100% complete for a piece of work. The more hand-offs, the more waste.
5. Task Switching	There are two aspects to it—first is the pure cost of the task switch (starting at 20% and increasing). Next is the dilution of focus for creative solutions within your knowledge workers.
6. Delays	Typically associated with organizational or process delays, for example—signing off documents, waiting for a document review, or software inspection by a SME—all of these time lags are wasteful.
7. Defects	Bugs, defects, or issues are pure waste. Even more insidious is the increased cost associated with them the later they are found and repaired.

Appendix D

References

Websites

- Agile Project Leadership Network – www.apln.org
- Agile Alliance – www.agilealliance.org
- Scrum Alliance – www.scrumalliance.org
- Poppendieck's Lean website – www.poppendieck.com
- Crystal – http://www.agilekiwi.com/crystal_clear.htm, http://crystalmethodologies.org,
- Scrum – www.controlchaos.com, Scrum, Stories - www.mountaingoatsoftware.com, www.scrumalliance.org, www.implementingscrum.com
- Scrum Search – http://scrumoogle.com
- Planning Poker - http://www.planningpoker.com/
- XP – www.extremeprogramming.org, www.xprogramming.com,
- Agile Journal – www.agilejournal.com
- CM Crossroads – www.cmcrossroads.com
- Lean - http://leanagile.blogspot.com
- Ward Cunningham's FIT site – http://fit.c2.com/ and FIT Book materials – http://fit.c2.com/wiki.cgi?FitBook
- FITLibrary - http://sourceforge.net/projects/fitlibrary, http://fitnesse.org/FitNesse.FitLibraryUserGuide
- FitNesse - http://fitnesse.org/, http://fitnesse.org/FitNesse.UserGuide
- Pragmatic Marketing – www.pragmaticmarketing.com

Alistair Cockburn discussion surrounding using Use Cases over User Stories – http://alistair.cockburn.us/Why+I+still+use+use+cases

Discussion Groups

- Agile Testing – http://tech.groups.yahoo.com/group/agile-testing/
- Scrum Development – http://groups.yahoo.com/group/scrumdevelopment/

- **Net Objectives / Shalloway LEAN and Scrum** –
  http://tech.groups.yahoo.com/group/leanagilescrum/
- **Poppendieck LEAN group** –
  http://tech.groups.yahoo.com/group/leandevelopment/

Books

I consider this a very short list of practical books that provide guidance that is relevant for the Great Product Owner. Every one of these should be on your bookshelf!

- **Cohn, Mike, "User Stories Applied – For Agile Software Development", Addison Wesley, 2004**
- **Cohn, Mike, "Agile Estimating and Planning", Addison Wesley, 2006**
- **Kniberg, Henrik, "Scrum and XP From the Trenches", www.lulu.com, 2006**
- **Larman, Craig, "Agile and Iterative Development – A Manager's Guide", Addison Wesley, 2004**
- **Leffingwell, Dean, "Scaling Software Agility – Best Practices for Large Enterprises", Addison Wesley, 2007**
- **Schwaber, Ken, "Agile Project Management with Scrum", Microsoft Press, 2004**

There are two additional books that I think can help you beyond the 'basics' and move you towards working more effectively within your organization and teams—

- **Manns, Mary Lynn and Rising, Linda, Fearless Change – Patterns for Introducing New Ideas", Addison Wesley, 2004**
- **Tabaka, Jean, "Collaboration Explained – Facilitation Skills for Software Project Leaders", Addison Wesley, 2006**

Videos

Many of the key thought leaders within the agile community have produced videos that are freely available on the web. For example, Mike Cohn has several estimation videos on Google video, as do others. Search for Schwaber, Sutherland, Agile Methods, Agile Testing, etc. for a relatively rich set of learning resources.

Author Background

Bob Galen is President of RGalen Consulting Group, LLC. a North Carolina based firm specializing in the strategy development, coaching & training of teams making the organizational shift towards Scrum and the other Agile methods and practices. Bob has held director, manager and contributor level positions in both software development and quality assurance organizations. He has over 25 years of experience working in a wide variety of domains at companies including—Bayer, Bowe–Bell & Howell Mail Processing, ChannelAdvisor, EMC, Lucent, Unisys and Thomson.

Since 2001, RGCG has provided consulting and training services targeted toward the *softer side* of software project challenges and improving team skills to deliver great products. This focus synergizes incredibly well with the Agile Methodologies and their practices.

Bob is an active member of ACM, IEEE/CS, PMI, QAI and SPIN. He regularly speaks at international conferences (Agile, STAR, Software Development, PSQT/PSTT, Better Software, and QAI) and to local Southeastern US organizations on topics related to software development, project management, software testing and team leadership.

He is a Certified Scrum Master Practicing (CSP) since 2004, Certified Scrum Product Owner (CSPO), and an active member of the Agile Alliance & Scrum Alliance. In 2005 he published the book *Software Endgames – Eliminating Defects, Controlling Change and the Countdown to On-Time Delivery* with Dorset House. The books' focus is how to successfully *finish* your software projects.

This is his second book. He's currently working on a third focused on Agile Project Estimation & Planning.

Bob may be reached directly at – bob@rgalen.com or for more background information and to check on his whereabouts see – www.rgalen.com